THE FOUR
NOBLE TRUTHS

THE FOUR
NOBLE TRUTHS

Fundamentals of the Buddhist Teachings
His Holiness the XIV Dalai Lama

translated by Geshe Thupten Jinpa
edited by Dominique Side

HarperCollins *Publishers* India
a joint venture with

New Delhi

HarperCollins *Publishers* India
a joint venture with
The India Today Group
by arrangement with
HarperCollins *Publishers* Limited

First published in 1958

First published in 1998 by
HarperCollins *Publishers* India

Eleventh impression 2006

ISBN-13: 978-81-7223-551-2
ISBN-10: 81-7223-551-8

HarperCollins *Publishers*
1A Hamilton House, Connaught Place, New Delhi 110 001, India
77-85 Fulham Palace Road, London W6 8JB, United Kingdom
Hazelton Lanes, 55 Avenue Road, Suite 2900, Toronto, Ontario M5R 3L2
and 1995 Markham Road, Scarborough, Ontario M1B 5M8, Canada
25 Ryde Road, Pymble, Sydney, NSW 2073, Australia
31 View Road, Glenfield, Auckland 10, New Zealand
10 East 53rd Street, New York NY 10022, USA

Printed and bound at
Thomson Press (India) Ltd.

CONTENTS

PREFACE

In July 1996, His Holiness the Dalai Lama
gave a series of lectures on Buddhist thought
and practice at the Barbican Centre in London.
These talks were facilitated by the Network
of Buddhist Organisations in U.K. – a national
association of Buddhist Centres.

The central theme of His Holiness the Dalai
Lama's lectures at the Barbican Centre, which
form the core of this book, is the Buddhist
teaching on the principle of the Four Noble
Truths, which is the foundation of all Buddha's
teachings. In these talks, His Holiness presents
a comprehensive explanation of the subject,
helping us to gain a better understanding of
the Four Noble Truths.

The appendix, 'Compassion – the Basis for
Human Happiness', is the text of a general

public talk by His Holiness at the Free Trade Centre in Manchester. This was organized by the Tibet Society of U.K. – which is one of the oldest Tibetan Support organizations. This chapter on compassion complements the teachings on the Four Noble Truths beautifully as it illustrates how the teachings of the Buddha can be applied in our day-to-day life.

As His Holiness the Dalai Lama's central message in these talks is compassion and the teachings on how to live a life of human kindness, it is our hope that this book will be of interest and benefit to people of all faiths and also those who do not share in any religious faiths.

The Office of Tibet in London would like to thank Cait Collins and Jane Rasch for transcribing the tapes of the talks, and Dominique Side and the translator Geshe Thupten Jinpa for editing the manuscript for publication.

Kesang Y. Takla (Mrs)
Representative of H. H. the Dalai Lama
London

INTRODUCTION

The Four Noble Truths are the very foundation of the Buddhist teaching, and that is why they are so important. In fact, if you don't understand the Four Noble Truths, and if you have not experienced the truth of this teaching personally, it is impossible to practise Buddha Dharma. Therefore I am always very happy to have the opportunity to explain them.

Generally speaking, I believe that all the major world religions have the potential to serve humanity and develop good human beings. By 'good' or 'nice', I don't mean that people look good; I mean that they have a good and more compassionate heart. This is why I always say that it is better to follow one's own traditional religion, because by changing religion you may eventually find emotional or intellectual difficulties. For

1

example, here in England the traditional religious culture is Christian, so it may be better for you to follow that.

However, for those of you who really feel that your traditional religion is not effective for you, and for those who are radical atheists, then the Buddhist way of explaining things may hold some attraction. Maybe in this case it is all right to follow Buddhism – generally, I think it is better to have some kind of religious training than none at all. If you really feel attracted to the Buddhist approach, and the Buddhist way of training the mind, it is very important to reflect carefully, and only when you feel it is really suitable for you is it right to adopt Buddhism as your personal religion.

There is another very important point here. Human nature is such that sometimes, in order to justify our adoption of a new religion, we may criticize our previous religion, or our country's traditional religion, and claim it is inadequate. This should not happen. Firstly, although your previous religion may not be effective for you, that does not mean it will completely fail to be of value to millions of other people. Since we should respect all human beings, we must also respect those who are following different religious paths. Furthermore, your previous religion – like all religions – does have the potential to help certain types of people. It is clear that for some people the Christian approach is more effective than the Buddhist one. It depends on the individual's mental disposition. We must therefore appreciate that potential in each religion, and respect all those who follow them.

The second reason is that we are now becoming aware of the many religious traditions of the world, and people are trying to promote genuine harmony between them. One example of this is the interfaith gathering in Assisi in 1986[1] on religions and the environment. I think there are now many interfaith circles and the idea of religious pluralism is taking root. This is a very encouraging sign. At such a time, when people are promoting genuine religious understanding in many areas, a single individual's criticism can be very harmful. So on these grounds, we should maintain a spirit of respect for other religions.

I wanted to begin with these points, because when I actually explain the Four Noble Truths, I have to argue the Buddhist way is the best! Also, if you were to ask me what the best religion is for me personally, my answer would be Buddhism, without any hesitation. But that does not mean that Buddhism is best for everyone – certainly not. Therefore, during the course of my explanation, when I say that I feel that the Buddhist way is best, you should not misunderstand me.

I would like to further emphasize that when I say that all religions have great potential, I am not just being polite or diplomatic. Whether we like it or not, the entire human race cannot be Buddhist, that is quite clear. Similarly, the whole of humanity cannot be Christian, or Muslim, either. Even in India during the Buddha's time, the entire population did not turn to Buddhism. This is just a fact. Furthermore, I have not just read books about other religions but I have met genuine practitioners from other traditions. We have talked about deep, spiritual experiences, in particular the experience of loving kindness. I have noticed a genuine and very forceful loving kindness in their minds. My conclusion therefore is that these various religions have the potential to develop a good heart.

Whether or not we like the philosophy of other religions isn't really the point. For a non-Buddhist, the idea of nirvana and a next life seems nonsensical. Similarly, to Buddhists the idea of a Creator God sometimes sounds like nonsense. But these things don't matter; we can drop them. The point is that through these different traditions, a very negative person can be transformed into a good person. That is the purpose of religion – and that is the actual result. This alone is a sufficient reason to respect other religions.

There is one last point. As you may know, Buddha taught in different ways, and Buddhism has a variety of philosophical systems such as Vaibhashika, Sautrantika, Chittamatra and Madhyamaka. Each one of these schools quotes the word of the Buddha from the Sutras. If the Buddha taught in these different ways, it would seem that he himself was not very sure about how things really are! But this is not actually the case; the Buddha knew the different mental dispositions of his followers. The main purpose of teaching religion is to help people, not to become famous, so he taught what was suitable according to the disposition of his listeners. So even Buddha Shakyamuni very much respected the views and rights of individuals. A teaching may be very profound but if it does not suit a particular person, what is the use of explaining it? In this sense, the Dharma is like medicine. The main value of medicine is that it cures illness; it is not just a question of price. For example, one medicine may be very precious and expensive, but if it is not appropriate for the patient, then it is of no use.

Since there are different types of people in the world, we need different types of religion. Let me give you one example of this. At the beginning of the 70s, an Indian engineer showed a keen interest in Buddhism and eventually became a monk. He was very sincere and a very nice person. Then one day I explained to him the Buddhist theory of *anatman*, the theory of no-self or no-soul,[2] and he was so frightened by it he was shaking all over. If there really was no permanent soul, then he felt there was something very fundamental missing. He was literally shivering all over. I found it very difficult to explain the meaning of anatman to him; it took months. Eventually his shivering grew less and less. So for such a person, it is better to practise a teaching that is based on atman, or a belief in the soul.

If we are aware of all these points, then it is very easy to respect and appreciate the value of traditions other than our own.

BASIC PRINCIPLES OF BUDDHISM

Whenever I introduce the Buddhist teachings, I make a point of presenting them in terms of two basic principles. The first of these is the interdependent nature of reality.[3] All Buddhist philosophy rests on an understanding of this basic truth. The second principle is that of non-violence, which is the action taken by a Buddhist practitioner who has the view of the interdependent nature of reality. Non-violence essentially means that we should do our best to help others and, if this is not possible, should at the very least refrain from harming them. Before I explain the Four Noble Truths in detail, I propose to outline both these principles by way of background.

Taking Refuge and Generating Bodhichitta

First, I will introduce these principles in traditional Buddhist terms. Technically, we become a Buddhist when we decide to take Refuge in the Three Jewels, and when we generate *bodhichitta*, which is known as compassion, the altruistic mind, or our good heart. The Three Jewels of Buddhism are the Buddha; the Dharma, his teaching; and the Sangha or community of practitioners. It is very clear that the idea of helping others lies at the heart of both Refuge and Bodhichitta. The practice of Generating Bodhichitta explicitly entails committing oneself to activities which are primarily aimed at helping others; while the practice of Taking Refuge lays the foundation for the practitioner to lead his or her life in an ethically disciplined way, avoiding actions that are harmful to others and respecting the laws of karma.

Unless we have a good foundational experience of the practice of Taking Refuge in the

Three Jewels, we will not be able to have a high level of realization of bodhichitta. It is for this reason that the distinction between a practising Buddhist and a non-Buddhist is made on the basis of whether or not an individual has taken Refuge in the Three Jewels.

However, when we talk about Taking Refuge in the Three Jewels, we should not imagine that it simply involves a ceremony in which we formally take Refuge from a master, or that merely by virtue of participating in such a ceremony we have become a Buddhist. There is a formal Refuge ceremony in Buddhism, but the ceremony is not the point. The point is that as a result of your own reflection, even without a master, you become fully convinced of the validity of the Buddha, Dharma and Sangha as the true ultimate objects of refuge, and that is when you actually become a Buddhist. You entrust your spiritual wellbeing to the Three Jewels, and this is what is really meant by Taking Refuge. On the other hand, if there is any doubt or apprehension in your mind about the validity of Buddha, Dharma and Sangha as being the ultimate objects of refuge, even though you may have taken part in a Refuge ceremony, that very suspicion or doubt prevents you from being a practising Buddhist, at least for the time being. It is therefore important to understand what these objects of refuge are.

When we speak about Buddha in this context, we should not confine our understanding of the word to the historical person who came to India and taught a certain spiritual way of life. Rather, our understanding of buddhahood[4] should be based on levels of consciousness, or levels of spiritual realization. We should understand that buddhahood is a spiritual state of being. This is why the Buddhist scriptures can speak about past buddhas, buddhas of the present and buddhas of the future.

Now the next question is: how does a buddha come into being? How does a person become fully enlightened? When we reflect on buddhahood, we are bound to ask ourselves whether or not it is possible for an individual to attain such a state, to become a fully enlightened being, a buddha. Here we find that the key lies in understanding the nature of Dharma. If the Dharma exists, then the Sangha will certainly exist – the Sangha are those who have engaged in the path of the Dharma, and who have realized and actualized its truth. If there are Sangha members who have reached spiritual states where they have overcome at least the gross levels of negativity and afflictive emotions, then we can envision the possibility of attaining a freedom from negativity and afflictive emotions which is total. That state is what we call buddhahood.

In the present context, I think we must make a distinction between the use of 'Dharma' as a generic term and its use in the specific framework of the Refuge. Generically, it refers to the scriptural Dharma – the Buddha's teaching and the spiritual realizations based on the practice of that teaching. In relation to the Refuge it has two aspects: one is the path that leads to the cessation of suffering and afflictive emotions, and the other is cessation⁵ itself. It is only by understanding true cessation and the path leading to cessation that we can have some idea of what the state of liberation is.

Dependent Origination

In the Sutras, Buddha stated several times that whoever perceives the interdependent nature of reality sees the Dharma; and whoever sees the Dharma sees the Buddha.[6] It is my belief that if we approach this statement from the perspective of Nagarjuna's teachings of the Madhyamaka School, we can arrive at the most comprehensive understanding of its implications. If you were to accuse me of having a bias in favour of Nagarjuna, I would certainly accept that criticism! So following Nagarjuna, we find there are three levels of meaning here.

Firstly, the understanding of the principle of interdependent origination (*pratityasamutpada*) that is common to all Buddhist schools explains it in terms of causal dependence. 'Pratit' means 'to depend on', and 'samutpada' refers to 'origination'. This principle means that all conditioned things and events in the universe come into being only as a result of the interaction of various causes and conditions. This is significant because it precludes two possibilities. One is the possibility that things can arise from nowhere, with no causes and conditions, and the second is that things can arise on account of a transcendent designer or creator. Both these possibilities are negated.

Secondly, we can understand the principle of dependent origination in terms of parts and whole. All material objects can be understood in terms of how the parts compose the whole, and how the very idea of 'whole' and 'wholeness' depends upon the existence of parts. Such dependence clearly exists in the physical world. Similarly, non-physical entities, like consciousness, can be considered in terms of their temporal sequences: the idea of their unity or wholeness is based upon the successive sequences that compose a continuum. So when we consider the universe in these terms, not only do we see each conditioned thing as dependently originated, we also understand that the entire phenomenal world arises according to the principle of dependent origination.

There is a third dimension to the meaning of dependent origination, which is that all things and events – everything, in fact – arise solely as a result of the mere coming together of the many factors which make them up. When you analyse things by mentally breaking them down into their constitutive parts, you come to the understanding that it is simply in dependence upon other factors that anything comes into being. Therefore there is nothing that has any independent or intrinsic identity of its own. Whatever identity we give things is contingent on the interaction between our perception and reality itself. However, this is not to say that things do not exist. Buddhism is not nihilistic. Things do exist, but they do not have an independent, autonomous reality.

Let us now refer back to the statement by the Buddha, when he said that seeing dependent origination leads to seeing the Dharma. There are three different meanings to this concept of Dharma which correspond to the three different levels of meaning of dependent origination which we have just described.

Firstly, we can relate Dharma to the first level of meaning of dependent origination, which is causal dependence. By developing a deep understanding of the interdependent nature of reality in terms of causal dependence, we are able to appreciate the workings of what we call 'karma', that is, the karmic law of cause and effect which governs human actions. This law explains how experiences of pain and suffering arise as a result of negative actions, thoughts and behaviour, and how desirable experiences such as happiness and joy arise as a result of the causes and conditions which correspond to that result – positive actions, emotions and thoughts.

Developing a deep understanding of dependent origination in terms of causal dependence gives you a fundamental insight into the nature of reality. When you realize that everything we perceive and experience arises as a result of the interaction and coming together of causes and conditions, your whole view changes. Your perspective on your own inner experiences, and the world at large, shifts as you begin to see everything in terms of this causal principle. Once you have developed that kind of philosophical outlook, then you will be able to situate your understanding of karma within that framework, since the karmic laws are a particular instance of this overall general causal principle.

Similarly, when you have a deep understanding of the other two dimensions of dependent origination – the dependence of parts and whole, and the interdependence between perception and existence – your view will deepen, and you will appreciate that there is a disparity between the way things appear to you and the way they actually are. What appears as some kind of autonomous, objective reality out there does not really fit with the actual nature of reality.

Once we appreciate that fundamental disparity between appearance and reality, we gain a certain insight into the way our emotions work, and how we react to events and objects. Underlying the strong emotional responses we have to situations, we see that there is an assumption that some kind of independently existing reality exists out there. In this way, we develop an insight into the various functions of the mind and the different levels of consciousness within us. We also grow to understand that although certain types of mental or emotional states seem so real, and although objects appear to be so vivid, in reality they are mere illusions.

They do not really exist in the way we think they do.

It is through this type of reflection and analysis that we will be able to gain an insight into what in technical Buddhist language is called 'the origin of suffering', in other words, those emotional experiences that lead to confusion and misapprehension, and which afflict the mind. When this is combined with an understanding of the interdependent nature of reality at the subtlest level, then we also gain insight into what we call 'the empty nature of reality', by which we mean the way each and every object and event arises only as a combination of many factors, and has no independent or autonomous existence.

Our insight into emptiness will, of course, help us to understand that any ideas that are based on the contrary view, that things exist intrinsically and independently, are misapprehensions. They are misunderstandings of the nature of reality. We realize that they have no valid grounding either in reality or in our own valid experience, whereas the empty nature of reality has a valid grounding both in logical reasoning and in our experience.

Gradually, we come to appreciate that it is possible to arrive at a state of knowledge where such misapprehension is eliminated completely; that is the state of cessation.

In *Clear Words* (*Prasannapada*), Chandrakirti states that if one can posit emptiness, then one can posit the world of dependent origination. If one can posit that, then one can posit the causal relationship between suffering and its origin. Once one accepts this, then one can also conceive of and accept the possibility that there could be an end to suffering. If one can do that, argues Chandrakirti, then one can also accept that it is possible for individuals to realize and actualize that state. Finally, of course, one can conceive of buddhas who have actually perfected that state of cessation.

The point is that by developing a profound understanding of the principle of dependent origination, we can understand both the truth of the subtle origins of suffering, and the truth of cessation. This is the meaning of Buddha's statement, that by understanding dependent origination, we see the Dharma. In this way we can see the truth of cessation and the path that leads to that cessation. Once we understand these, we are able to conceive that it is possible for Sangha members to realize and actualize these states, and for buddhas to perfect them. Finally, we come to some understanding of what buddhahood really means.

The Two Truths

Now in order to develop a comprehensive understanding of the Four Noble Truths, I think it is also necessary to be familiar with the Two Truths, conventional or relative truth, and ultimate truth. Here you must keep in mind that I explain them from the perspective of the Madhyamaka or 'Middle Way' School of Buddhism. Of course, the concept of Two Truths is not confined to this school alone. You can find the concept of Two Truths in other Buddhist schools of thought, and also in some non-Buddhist Indian philosophies. Here, however, I take the Madhyamaka view.

So how can we develop a personal understanding of the fundamental Buddhist doctrine of the Two Truths? By coming to know our everyday world of lived experience, we appreciate what is known as *samvaharasatya*, the world of conventional reality, where the causal principle operates. If we accept the reality of this world as conventional, then we can accept the empty nature of this world which, according to Buddhism, is the ultimate truth, the *paramarthasatya*. The relationship between these two aspects of reality is important. The world of appearance is used not so much as a contrast or an opposite to the world of ultimate truth, but rather as the evidence, the very basis on which the ultimate nature of reality is established.

Only when you have an understanding of the nature and relationship of these Two Truths are you in a position to fully understand the meaning of the Four Noble Truths. And once you understand the Four Noble Truths, then you have a sound foundation on which to develop a good understanding of what is meant by Taking Refuge in the Three Jewels.

QUESTIONS

Q: What is the difference between individuals gaining insights and the buddhas' perfection of those insights?

HHDL: Let us take the example of gaining insight into the subtle impermanence and momentary nature of all things and events.

For an individual who starts with an understanding of things as being permanent, at the initial stage his or her grasping at the permanence of things could be quite strong and intense. Now in order to loosen that grip you need some form of critical reasoning which, even if it only casts a doubt in the person's mind as to the permanence of things, can in itself make an impact because it has at least had the effect of loosening the grip on the idea that things are permanent or eternal.

However, that is not enough. You need the further reinforcement of more critical reasoning to point you towards the impermanence of things. Even that is not enough. You will need yet more conviction than this, and that can be gained through constant reflection, which can lead to what is known as the inferential understanding of impermanence.

The process is not over yet. For this understanding to have a definite impact on your
behaviour, you need to gain direct insight, or
intuitive experience, of the impermanence of
things. That in turn needs to be further perfected, because the point is that our grasping
at permanence is so deeply embedded in our
consciousness that just one single insight is
not enough to dispel it. It requires a long
process of deepening our insight, so that eventually even the smallest tendency to grasp at
permanence has been eradicated.

The process would be the same in the case
of insight into the emptiness of things, or of
any other principle in fact.

However, there are certain aspects of the
spiritual path which have less to do with
experiences related to knowledge, and more
to do with the enhancement of our good heart.
For the latter, at the initial stage, you have
to develop some intellectual understanding
of what compassion is, of course, and you
have to have some notion of how it could
be enhanced. Then, as a result of your practice, you may gain some kind of simulated

experience of your good heart. For example, when you sit and reflect on it, you may arouse your compassion, but that compassion is not long-lasting or pervasive, and does not permeate your very being. So what is needed is a further deepening of that experience so that your compassion becomes spontaneous, so it is no longer dependent upon intellectual simulation. It has to become a truly spontaneous response to occasions that demand that response. That experience of compassion can be further deepened again, until it becomes universal. So this is a different aspect of the path, which again entails a long process.

These two aspects of the path are known in traditional Buddhist terms as the Method Aspect and the Insight or Wisdom Aspect, and both must go hand in hand. For insight to be enhanced and deepened, you need the complementary factor of bodhichitta from the Method Aspect. Similarly, in order to enhance, deepen and strengthen your realization of bodhichitta, you need the insight which grounds it. So we need an approach which combines method and wisdom.

Likewise we need an approach which combines several different methods, not an approach which relies on only one. If we take the previous case of insight into the impermanence of things, although that insight might in itself enable a person to overcome grasping at permanence, in practice you need further complementary factors in order to perfect that particular insight. This is because there are so many other fetters that constrict the mind at the same time. The person's problem is not just grasping at permanence in isolation; it is also grasping at the independent, objective reality of things, like grasping at abiding principles, and so on and so forth. All these factors can be counteracted together by developing insight into emptiness.

So what we are dealing with here is the very complex process of the progression of an individual's consciousness towards perfection.

Q: Can you say more about exactly what is meant by Going for Refuge?

HHDL: I feel that the essence of Going for Refuge is the development of a deep conviction in the efficacy of the Dharma as a means to liberation, as well as a deep aspiration or desire to attain that liberation.

Generally speaking, Buddha is said to be the teacher who shows us the path, Dharma is the actual object of Refuge, and the Sangha are your companions on the path. So therefore a deep conviction in the Dharma is a precondition for developing deep faith and respect in the Buddha and the Sangha.

In his Commentary on the *Compendium of Valid Cognition* (*Pramanavarttika*), Dharmakirti tries to rationally prove the validity and reliability of the fact that Buddha is an enlightened teacher. He defends his argument by subjecting Buddha's own teaching to profound scrutiny, and by demonstrating the reliability of his teaching on the Four Noble Truths because it is grounded in both reasoning and valid personal experience. The point here is that we should first appreciate the truth of the Dharma, and only on that basis recognize the Buddha as a genuine teacher.

Only in relation to extremely obscure areas is the reverse logic sometimes applied; in other words, that Buddha's statements on such matters can be relied upon *because* he is a reliable teacher. This is a complex process of reasoning. In order to follow it, we actually proceed from our own conviction in the reliability of Buddha's teachings on the Four Noble Truths, which are open to critical reasoning. When we have gained personal insight into the truth of these, we develop a deep conviction in the reliability of Buddha as a teacher. Since Buddha has proven to be reliable and rational in areas that are open to reason, we have the confidence to take Buddha's testimony on trust in other areas which we find more obscure.

Taking Refuge in the Three Jewels therefore derives its full meaning from the act of Taking Refuge in the Dharma.

Q: What is the purpose of Taking Refuge in a ritual or ceremony if one can take refuge within one's own heart alone?

HHDL: In Buddhism we have a number of different precepts or vows. For example, there are bodhisattva vows, tantric vows, pratimoksha vows (monastic vows), lay person's precepts, and so on. It is said that you can take bodhisattva vows in front of a representation of the Buddha (a statue or painting, for example) and do not need to take them from another living person. However, it is necessary to take Vajrayana and pratimoksha vows from another living person, because you need an unbroken continuum. Perhaps one of the reasons for this is that taking vows in the presence of a master or other living person brings a greater sense of commitment. It reinforces your own conscience, and gives a sense of personal obligation. If you wish to pursue the reasons for this further, then I must admit we would have to defer the question to the Buddha himself.

Q: If we see someone engaging in a wrong action which will lead to their suffering, should we try to prevent them from carrying it out, or would that be imposing on their karma? In other words, is it better for us to experience our own suffering so we can learn from it?

HHDL: As you know, a practising Buddhist is deliberately engaged in a way of life that is dedicated to helping others. Here we should know that, in the Buddhist sense, we are talking about helping others find their own liberation through engaging in the right path; that is, engaging in a way of life that accords with the karmic law, where the person avoids negative actions and engages in positive actions. So generally speaking, when a Buddhist sees others engaging in wrong actions, it is right to try to stop them from doing so.

However, this does raise several questions. To what extent can we impose our own morality, or our own sets of values, on to another person? We might even wonder whether the Buddha's prescription to his followers to live their lives according to the moral discipline of avoiding the Ten Negative Actions[7] is also a way of imposing *his* set of moral values on us.

It is useful to remember that one important principle in Buddhism is the need to be sensitive to individual context. There is a story which illustrates this point well.

Shariputra, one of the chief disciples of the Buddha, knew that if he were to give the basic teachings on the Shravakayana to a group of five hundred potential disciples, these disciples would without doubt gain insight into the truth and become Arhats. However, the bodhisattva named Manjushri intervened, and instead taught them the Mahayana doctrine of emptiness. These five hundred disciples understood what he taught as a doctrine of total nihilism, denying the validity and reality of everything. They all developed wrong views on the nature of the path and reality, and as a result it is said that they created karmic actions that led them to take rebirth in the lower realms of existence.

So Shariputra sought out the Buddha straightaway, arguing that if Manjushri had let him guide these five hundred people, they would have at least attained high levels of realization, if not full enlightenment. The Buddha responded by saying that in fact Manjushri had applied the principle of skilful means. Manjushri knew that in the short term these people would create negative actions through their wrong views, but he also knew that because the doctrine of emptiness had been implanted in their consciousness, those seeds would later ripen and would lead them to buddhahood. So in effect, their path to buddhahood had been shortened.

The moral that we can draw from this story is that until we reach the state of full enlightenment ourselves, it is very difficult to judge what is, and what is not, the right response to a given situation. We should simply do our best to be sensitive to each particular situation when we are interacting with others.

Q: Your Holiness, it is a well-known fact that you are a very busy person with many demands on your time. Could you advise a lay person with home, family and work demands, on how to develop a systematic pattern of Dharma practice?

HHDL: My Western friends often ask me for the quickest, easiest, most effective – and cheapest – way of practising Dharma! I think to find such a way is impossible! Maybe that is a sign of failure!

We should realize that practising the Dharma is actually something that needs to be done twenty-four hours of the day. That's why we make a distinction between actual meditation sessions and post-meditation periods, the idea being that both while you are in the meditative session and also when you are out of it, you should be fully within the realm of Dharma practice.

In fact, one could say that the post-meditation periods are the real test of the strength of your practice. During formal meditation, in a sense you are recharging your batteries, so that when you come out of the session you are better equipped to deal with the demands of your everyday life. The very purpose of recharging a battery is to enable it to run something, isn't it? Similarly, once you have equipped yourself through whatever practices you engage in, as a human being you can't avoid the daily routines of life, and it is during these periods that you should be able to live according to the principles of your Dharma practice.

Of course at the initial stage, as a beginner, you do need periods of concentrated meditation so that you have a base from which you can begin. This is certainly crucial. But once you have established that base, then you will be able to adopt a way of life where your daily activity is at least in accord with the principles of the Dharma. So all this points to the importance of making an effort. Without some effort, there is no way that we can integrate the principles of Dharma in our lives.

For a serious practitioner, the most serious effort is necessary. Just a few short prayers, a little chanting, and some mantra recitation with a mala (rosary) are not sufficient. Why not? Because this cannot transform your mind. Our negative emotions are so powerful that constant effort is needed in order to counteract them. If we practise constantly, then we can definitely change.

Q: What is the relationship between relative compassion and absolute compassion?

HHDL: There are different ways of understanding the meaning of compassion according to whether you approach it from the Mahayana or the Vajrayana point of view. For example, although the Vajrayana uses the same word for compassion, *karuna*, as the Mahayana, it has a totally different meaning.

Perhaps this question is related to another distinction made in the scriptures between two levels of compassion. At the first level, compassion is simulated. This is the initial

stage, when you need to practise certain con-
templations in order to generate compassion.
As a result of this practice you reach the
second level, at which compassion becomes
natural and spontaneous. This is one of the
ways of understanding the difference between
relative and absolute compassion.

ONE

INTRODUCING THE FOUR NOBLE TRUTHS

Now let us turn to the Buddhist teaching on the Four Noble Truths. The first question we might ask is why these Truths are considered to be so fundamental, and why, in fact, Buddha taught them at all.

In order to answer this, we have to relate the Four Noble Truths to our own experience as individual human beings. It is a fact – a natural fact of life – that each one of us has an innate desire to seek happiness and to overcome suffering. This is something very instinctive, and there is no need to prove it is there. Happiness is something that we all aspire to achieve, and of course we naturally have a right to fulfil that aspiration. In the same way, suffering is something everybody wishes to avoid, and we also have the right to try to overcome suffering. So if this aspiration to achieve happiness and overcome suffering is our natural state of being, and our natural quest, the question is how we should go about fulfilling that aspiration.

This leads us to the teachings on the Four Noble Truths, which provide an understanding of the relationship between two sets of events: causes and their effects. On one side we have suffering, but suffering does not come from nowhere, it arises as a result of its own causes and conditions. On the other side we have happiness, which also arises from its own particular set of causes and conditions.

Now when we speak of happiness in Buddhism, our understanding of it is not confined to a state of feeling. Certainly cessation (the total cessation of suffering) is not a state of feeling, and yet we could say that cessation is the highest form of happiness because it is, by definition, complete freedom from suffering. Here again cessation, or true happiness, does not come into being from nowhere or without any cause. This is a subtle point, of course, because from the Buddhist perspective cessation is not a conditioned event, so it cannot be said to be actually produced, or caused, by anything. However, the actualization or attainment of cessation does depend on the path and on an individual's effort. You cannot attain cessation without making an effort. In this sense we can therefore say that the path that leads to cessation is the cause of cessation.

The teachings on the Four Noble Truths clearly distinguish two sets of causes and effects: those causes which produce suffering, and those which produce happiness. By showing us how to distinguish these in our own lives, the teachings aim at nothing less than to enable us to fulfil our deepest aspiration – to be happy and to overcome suffering.

Once we have realized that this is why Buddha taught the Four Noble Truths, we might go on to ask ourselves the reason for their specific sequence: why are the Four Noble Truths taught in a particular order, starting with suffering, continuing with the origin of suffering, and so on? On this point we should understand that the order in which the Four Noble Truths are taught has nothing to do with the order in which things arise in reality. Rather, it is related to the way an individual should go about practising the Buddhist path, and attain realizations based on that practice.

In the *Uttaratantra*, Maitreya states that there are four stages to curing an illness.

Just as the disease need be diagnosed, its cause eliminated, a healthy state achieved and the remedy implemented, so also should suffering, its causes, its cessation and the path be known, removed, attained and undertaken.[1]

Maitreya uses the analogy of a sick person to explain the way in which realizations based on the Four Noble Truths can be attained. In order for a sick person to get well, the first step is that he or she must know that he is ill, otherwise the desire to be cured will not arise. Once you have acknowledged that you are sick, then naturally you will try to find out what led to it and what makes your condition even worse. When you have identified these, you will gain an understanding of whether or not the illness can be cured, and a wish to be free from the illness will arise in you. In fact this is not just a mere wish, because once you have recognized the conditions that led to your illness, your desire to be free of it will be much stronger since that knowledge will give you a confidence and conviction that you can overcome the illness. With that conviction, you will want to take all the medications and remedies necessary.

In the same way, unless you know that you are suffering, your desire to be free from suffering will not arise in the first place. So the first step we must take as practising Buddhists is to recognize our present state as *duhkha* or suffering, frustration and unsatisfactoriness. Only then will we wish to look into the causes and conditions that give rise to suffering.

It is very important to understand the context of the Buddhist emphasis on recognizing that we are all in a state of suffering, otherwise there is a danger we could misunderstand the Buddhist outlook, and think that it involves rather morbid thinking, a basic pessimism and almost an obsessiveness about the reality of suffering. The reason why Buddha laid so much emphasis on developing insight into the nature of suffering is because there is an alternative – there is a way out, it is actually possible to free oneself from it. This is why it is so crucial to realize the nature of suffering, because the stronger and deeper your insight into suffering is, the stronger your aspiration to gain freedom from it becomes. So the Buddhist emphasis on the nature of suffering should be seen within this wider perspective, where there is an appreciation of the possibility of complete freedom from suffering. If we had no concept of liberation, then to spend so much time reflecting on suffering would be utterly pointless.

We could say that the two sets of causes and effects I mentioned earlier refer, on the one hand, to the process of an unenlightened existence, which relates to the causal chain between suffering and its origins, and, on the other hand, to the process of an enlightened existence which pertains to the causal links between the path and true cessation. When the Buddha elaborated on these two processes, he taught what is called the doctrine of the Twelve Links of Dependent Origination, or Twelve Nidanas.[2]

The nidanas are the Twelve Links in the cycle of existence, which goes from ignorance, to volition, to consciousness, and so on, all the way to old age and death. When the causal process of an unenlightened existence is described in detail – that is, a life which is led within the framework of suffering and its origin – then the sequence of the Twelve Links begins with ignorance, and proceeds with volition, consciousness and so on. This sequence describes how an individual sentient being, as a result of certain causes and conditions, enters into the process of unenlightened existence.

However, if that same individual engages in certain spiritual practices, he or she can reverse this process, and the alternative sequence is that of the process which leads to enlightenment. For example, if the continuum of ignorance comes to an end then the continuum of volitional actions will cease. If that ceases, then the consciousness that serves as the support for such actions will cease; and so on.

You can see that the teachings on the Twelve Links of Dependent Origination are in some sense an elaboration on the two sets of causes and conditions described by the Four Noble Truths.

TWO

THE TRUTH OF
SUFFERING

The first of the Four Noble Truths is the Truth
of Suffering.

The various philosophical schools of Buddhism interpret the word 'truth' in different
ways. For example, there is a fundamental
difference between the Prasangika-Madhyamaka school and the Shravakayana schools in
the way they distinguish ordinary beings from
Arya or superior beings. The Shravakayana
makes the distinction on the basis of whether
or not a person has gained direct intuitive
insight into the Four Noble Truths. The
Prasangika-Madhyamikas do not accept this
criterion, because they hold that even ordinary beings can have direct intuitive realizations of the Four Noble Truths. However, I
will not go into these arguments here because
it would complicate my explanation.

Instead, we will turn straightaway to the meaning of *duhkha* or suffering. In this context, duhkha is the ground or basis of painful experience, and refers generally to our state of existence as conditioned by karma, delusions and afflictive emotions. As Asanga states in the *Compendium of Knowledge* (*Abhidharmasamuchchaya*), the concept of duhkha must embrace both the environment where we live and the individual beings living within it.

THE THREE REALMS OF SUFFERING

In order to understand the environment in which unenlightened beings live, we must look briefly at Buddhist cosmology.[1] According to the Buddhist teachings, there are Three Realms of existence: the Desire Realm, the Form Realm, and the Formless Realm.[2]

The difficulty here, for most of us, is how to understand these Three Realms. In particular, how should we conceive of form realms and formless realms? It is not enough to simply say that Buddha talked about these in the scriptures — that alone is not a sufficient reason for a Buddhist to accept their existence. Perhaps the most helpful approach is to understand these realms in terms of different levels of consciousness. For example, according to Buddhism, the very distinction between enlightened existence and unenlightened existence is made on the basis of the respective levels of consciousness. A person whose mind is undisciplined and untamed is in the state of samsara or suffering; whereas someone whose mind is disciplined and tamed is in the state of nirvana, or ultimate peace.

We also find that the Buddhist distinction between ordinary and Arya beings is made on the basis of their respective levels of consciousness or realization. Anyone who has gained direct intuitive realization of emptiness, or the ultimate nature of reality, is said to be an Arya according to Mahayana, and anyone who has not gained that realization is called an ordinary being. In relation to the Three Realms, the subtler the level of consciousness an individual attains, the subtler the realm of existence he can inhabit.

For example, if a person's ordinary mode of being is very much within the context of desire and attachment — that is to say that he tends to develop attachment to whatever he perceives, like desirable forms or pleasant sensations and so on – then such attachment to physical objects, thought processes and sensory experiences leads to a form of existence which is confined within the Desire Realm, both now and in the future. At the same time, there are people who have transcended attachment to objects of immediate perception and to physical sensations, but who are attached to the inner states of joy or bliss. That type of person creates causes that will lead him or her to future rebirths where physical existence has a much more refined form.

Furthermore, there are those who have transcended attachment not only to physical sensations but to pleasurable inner sensations of joy and bliss, too. They tend more towards a state of equanimity. Their level of consciousness is much subtler than the other two, but they are still attached to a particular mode of being. The grosser levels of their mind can lead to the Fourth Level of the Form Realm, while the subtler attachment towards equanimity leads to the Formless Realms. So this is the way we relate the Three Realms to levels of consciousness.

On the basis of this cosmology, Buddhism talks about the infinite process of the universe, coming into being and going through a process of dissolution before again coming into being. This process has to be understood in relation to the Three Realms of existence. According to the Sarvastivadin Abhidharma literature[3] (the Buddhist discourses on metaphysics and psychology which serve as a reference in Tibetan Buddhism), it is from the Third Level of the Form Realm downwards that the world is subject to the continuous process of arising and dissolution. From the Fourth Level of the Form Realm upwards, which includes the Formless Realm, the world is beyond this process which we could call the evolution of the physical universe.

This infinite process of evolution is very similar to the modern scientific notion of the Big Bang. If the scientific cosmological theory of the Big Bang accepts only one Big Bang as

the beginning of everything, then of course
that would not fit with basic Buddhist cosmology. In this case, Buddhists would have to
bite their nails and come up with some way
of explaining how the Big Bang does not
contradict the Buddhist idea of the evolutionary process of the universe. However, if the
Big Bang theory does not entail only one Big
Bang at the beginning, but accepts a multi-
plicity of Big Bangs, then that would correspond very well to the Buddhist understanding of the evolutionary process.

The Sarvastivadin Abhidharma also discusses the precise ways in which the universe
dissolves at the end of each cycle. When the
physical universe is destroyed by fire it is
destroyed only below the first level of the
Form Realm; when it is destroyed by water it
dissolves from the second level of the Form
Realm downwards; when it is destroyed by
wind, it is destroyed from the third level of
the Form Realm downwards. In Buddhist
cosmology, therefore, the evolution of the
physical universe is understood in terms of
the four elements of fire, water, wind and
earth. In general, we usually add space to this

list, making a total of five elements. A complex discussion on the elemental mechanics of dissolution can be found not only in the Abhidharma but also in the *Uttaratantra*. These explanations seem to be very similar to modern scientific theories.

Having said this, what is stated in the Abhidharma literature does not always have to be taken literally. According to the Abhidharma, for example, the structure of the universe is based on the model of a Mount Meru in the centre, surrounded by four 'continents'. We also find that many of the Abhidharmic descriptions of the size of the sun and moon contradict modern scientific explanations. Given that scientific experiments have proved these claims to be wrong, we will have to accept the conclusion of the scientists on these points.

So here I have outlined very briefly how Buddhism understands the evolution of the physical universe, or, in a broad sense, the environment. As for the sentient beings that inhabit these environments, Buddhism accepts many different types. There are beings with bodily forms and beings which are perceived

as formless. Even in the world with which we are familiar, there are many beings which are perceptible to our senses and some which are not, like those of the spirit world for example.

Generally speaking, the Buddhist understanding is that birth as a human being is one of the most ideal forms of existence because it is conducive to practising Dharma. So compared to human beings, spirits would in fact be considered inferior because that form of existence is less effective for pursuing the practice of Dharma. Spirits may have certain abilities that are not open to us, like certain powers of precognition or some supernatural powers, but the fact remains that they are part of this world where human beings also live. All beings in this world are under the control of delusion and afflictive emotions. In some sense one could say that they are actually the products of delusion and afflictive emotions.

Lama Tsongkhapa describes very vividly the unenlightened existence of sentient beings in samsara. He uses the analogy of someone being tied up very tightly by the ropes of negative karma, delusions, afflictive emotions and

thoughts. Encased in this tight net of ego and
self-grasping, they are tossed around aimlessly
by the currents of fluctuating experiences, of
suffering and pain.[4] This is what samsaric life
is like.

THREE TYPES OF SUFFERING

So now the question is, what is duhkha?
What is suffering? Buddhism describes three
levels or types of suffering. The first is called
'the suffering of suffering', the second, 'the
suffering of change', and the third is 'the
suffering of conditioning'.

When we talk about the first type, the
suffering of suffering, we are talking in very
conventional terms of experiences which we
would all identify as suffering. These experiences are painful. In Buddhism there are four
main experiences of this type of suffering
which are considered to be fundamental to
life in samsara: the sufferings of birth, sickness, ageing and death. The significance of
recognizing these states as forms of suffering,
and the importance of this recognition as a

catalyst of the spiritual quest, is very strongly demonstrated in the Buddha's own life story. According to the story, when he was the young Prince Siddhartha, the Buddha is said to have caught sight of a sick person, an old person, and a dead person being carried away. The impact of seeing this suffering apparently led him to the realization that so long as he was not free of the infinite process of birth, he would always be subject to these other three sufferings. Later, the sight of a spiritual aspirant is supposed to have made the Buddha fully aware that there is a possibility of freedom from this cycle of suffering.

So in Buddhism there is an understanding that so long as we are subject to the process of rebirth, all other forms of suffering are natural consequences of that initial starting point. We could characterize our life as being within the cycle of birth and death, and sandwiched in between these two, as it were, are the various sufferings related to illness and ageing.

The second level of suffering, the suffering of change, refers to experiences we ordinarily identify as pleasurable. However, in reality, as long as we are in an unenlightened state, all our joyful experiences are tainted and ultimately bring suffering.

Why does Buddhism claim that experiences which are apparently pleasurable are ultimately states of suffering? The point is that we perceive them as states of pleasure or joy only because, in comparison to painful experiences, they appear as a form of relief. Their pleasurable status is only relative. If they were truly joyful states in themselves, then just as painful experiences increase the more we indulge in the causes that lead to pain, likewise, the more we engage in the causes that give rise to pleasurable experience, our pleasure or joy should intensify; but this is not the case.

On an everyday level, for example, when you have good food, nice clothes, attractive jewellery and so on, for a short time you feel really marvellous. Not only do you enjoy a feeling of satisfaction, but when you show your things to others, they share in it too. But then one day passes, one week passes, one month passes, and the very same object that once gave you such pleasure might simply cause you frustration. That is the nature of things – they change. The same also applies to fame. At the beginning you might think to yourself, 'Oh! I'm so happy! Now I have a good name, I'm famous!' But after some time, it could be that all you feel is frustration and dissatisfaction. The same sort of change can happen in friendships and in sexual relationships. At the beginning you almost go mad with passion, but later that very passion can turn to hatred and aggression, and, in the worst cases, even lead to murder. So that is the nature of things. If you look carefully, everything beautiful and good, everything that we consider desirable, brings us suffering in the end.

Finally, we come to the third type of suffering, the suffering of conditioning. This addresses the main question: why is this the nature of things? The answer is, because everything that happens in samsara is due to ignorance. Under the influence or control of ignorance, there is no possibility of a permanent state of happiness. Some kind of trouble, some kind of problem, always arises. So long as we remain under the power of ignorance, that is, our fundamental misapprehension or confusion about the nature of things, then sufferings come one after another, like ripples on water.

The third level of suffering, therefore, refers to the bare fact of our unenlightened existence, which is under the influence of this fundamental confusion and of the negative karmas to which confusion gives rise. The reason it is called the suffering of conditioning is because this state of existence serves as the basis not only for painful experiences in this life, but also for the causes and conditions of suffering in the future.

Dharmakirti's *Commentary on the Compendium of Valid Cognition* (*Pramanavarttika*) and Aryadeva's *Four Hundred Verses on the Middle Way* (*Chatuhshatakashastrakarika*) both offer a useful way of looking at this third level of suffering, and help deepen our understanding of it. Both works lay the emphasis on reflecting upon the subtle level of the transient, impermanent nature of reality.

It is important to bear in mind that there are two levels of meaning here. One can understand impermanence in terms of how something arises, stays for a while, and then disappears. This level of impermanence can be understood quite easily. We should add that on this level, the dissolution of something requires a secondary condition which acts as a catalyst to destroy its continuity. However, there is also a second, more subtle understanding of transience. From this more subtle perspective, the obvious process of change we have just described is merely the effect of a deeper, underlying and dynamic process of change. At a deeper level, everything is changing from moment to moment, constantly. This process of momentary change is not due to a secondary condition that arises to destroy something, but rather the very cause that led a thing to arise is also the cause of its destruction. In other words, within the cause of its origin lies the cause of its cessation.

Momentariness should thus be understood in two ways. First, in terms of the three moments of existence of any entity – in the first instant, it arises; in the second instant, it stays; in the third instant, it dissolves. Second, in terms of each instant itself. An instant is not static; as soon as it arises, it moves towards its own cessation.

Since everything arises complete from the outset, the birth of things comes together with the seed or potential for their dissolution. In this respect, one could say that their cessation does not depend on any secondary, further condition. Therefore, in Buddhism, all phenomena are said to be 'other-powered', that is, they are under the control of their causes.

Once you have developed this understanding of the transient nature of phenomena, you are able to situate the understanding you have of dukkha within that context, and reflect upon your life as an individual in this samsaric world. You know that since the world has come into being as a result of its own causes and conditions, it too must be other-powered. In other words, it must be under the control of the causal processes that led to its arising. However, in the context of samsara, the causes that we are referring to here are nothing other than our fundamental confusion or ignorance (*marigpa* in Tibetan), and the delusory states to which confusion gives rise. We know that so long as we are under the domination of this fundamental

confusion, there is no room for lasting joy or happiness. Of course, within the Three Realms there are states which are comparatively more joyful than others. However, so long as we remain within samsara, whether in the Form Realm, the Formless Realm or the Desire Realm, there is no scope for joy to be lasting. In the final analysis, we are in a state of duhkha. This is the meaning of the third type of suffering.

IGNORANCE

The Sanskrit word for ignorance or confusion is *avidya*, which literally means 'not know-ing'. There are several interpretations of what is meant by avidya according to the different philosophical schools and their various views of the fundamental Buddhist doctrine of *anat-man* or no-self. However, the general mean-ing that is common to all the schools is an understanding that there lies a fundamental ignorance at the root of our existence. The reason for this is quite simple. We all know from personal experience that what we deeply aspire to gain is happiness and what we try to avoid is suffering. Yet our actions and our behaviour only lead to more suffering and not to the lasting joy and happiness that we seek. This must surely mean that we are operating within the framework of ignorance. This is how we experience the fundamental confusion at the root of our life.

One way to reflect on the nature of duhkha, according to the traditional Buddhist teachings, is to reflect on the sufferings endured in each of the six 'realms' of the samsaric world system.[5] These include the hell realms, the animal realm, the realm of pretas or hungry ghosts, and so on. For some people, such reflections may spur them to deepen their quest for freedom from suffering. However, for many other people, including myself, it can be more effective to reflect on our own human suffering. Although Buddhism teaches that human life is one of the most positive of all forms of life, since human beings have the potential to gain perfect enlightenment, it is not always that joyful. We are subject to the unavoidable sufferings of birth, death, ageing and sickness. In addition, when one reflects on the fact that life is conditioned and dominated by confusion, and the delusory emotions and thoughts to which confusion gives rise, then for someone like myself it seems much more effective to recognize this than to think about the sufferings of other realms.

As I mentioned before, the Buddhist scriptures describe the causal process through which ignorance gives rise to volitional acts, which in turn give rise to a birth in one of the samsaric worlds, and so on, as the Twelve Links in the Chain of Dependent Origination. On this, Buddha made three observations. He said that:

> Because there is this, that ensues.
> Because this came into being, that came into being.
> Because there is fundamental ignorance, volitional acts come into being.[6]

When commenting upon these three statements, Asanga explains in the *Compendium of Knowledge* that Three Conditions are necessary for anything to arise, and I think an understanding of these would be useful here.

Because there is this, that ensues

Asanga explained that the significance of the first statement is that all phenomena come into being because they have causes. One could say there is an infinite causal chain. It is not as if there were a first cause, or a 'beginning' point in time, from which everything arose. Asanga referred to that observation as the **Condition of the Existence of a Cause**.

Because this came into being, that came into being

When commenting on the second statement, Asanga introduced what he called the **Condition of Impermanence**. The meaning of this is that the mere fact that something exists is not sufficient for it to produce an effect. For something to have the potential to produce an effect, it must itself be subject to causation; in other words, it must come into being itself as a result of other causes. Hence we have an infinity of causes. So mere existence alone does not give rise to consequences; a cause should not only exist, it

60

should also be impermanent and subject to causation.

Because there is fundamental ignorance, volitional acts come into being

Asanga's comment on this mentions a further qualification that is needed for a cause to produce an effect, which he calls the **Condition of Potentiality**. The idea is that it is not sufficient for a cause to exist and to be impermanent for it to produce a particular result. It is not the case that everything can produce everything or anything. There must be some kind of natural correlation between a cause and its effect. For example, because the nature of our life is suffering we desire happiness, yet out of ignorance we create more suffering for ourselves, and this is because suffering is the root of our life. The result we obtain thus correlates with its cause.

So to summarize, Three Conditions are necessary for anything to arise: a cause should exist, it should be impermanent, and it should correlate with the effect.

In view of this, how should we understand the causal relationship between, say, ignorance and volitional acts? Buddhism pursues a rigorous analysis of causal relationships in general, and the scriptures contain many discussions on the different types of causes and conditions. However, there are principally two types of cause; one is known as the material or substantial cause, and the other as the contributory cause. By material cause we mean the very stuff that turns into the effect, so we can talk for example about the physical continuum of a physical entity. Many other factors are necessary to allow the transition to take place between a cause and its effect, and these are called the contributory causes.

Furthermore, there are different ways in which conditions can effect a result. These have more to do with the complex functioning of the mind. The scriptures identify five types of condition, such as the objective condition, which refers to the object of perception; the sensory organs that give rise to sensory perception; the immediately preceding condition, which is the earlier continuum of your consciousness; and so on. So you can see that the Buddhist understanding of causation is highly complex.

Let us take the example of fire. What would the material cause of fire be? We could say that a potential exists within the fuel that is used to make a fire, which then becomes the fire. In the case of consciousness, the issue is more complex. For example, it is obvious that we need the physical sensory organs for sensory perceptions to take place. Of course, the physical basis of consciousness would also include the nervous system, although in the classic Buddhist scriptures there is hardly any discussion of this, and it is perhaps something that needs to be added to Buddhist theories of epistemology and psychology. However, the substantial cause of consciousness would not be these physical entities. It has to be understood in terms of its own continuum, be it in the form of a potential or propensity or whatever. This is a very difficult topic, but perhaps we can say that the substantial cause of consciousness can be understood as the continuum of the subtle consciousness, although we should be careful not to end up in a position which implies that the material cause of anything is exactly the same as the thing itself. This would be untenable. We cannot maintain the position, for instance, that the substantial causes of sensory perceptions are always sensory perceptions, because sensory consciousnesses are gross levels of consciousness and are contingent on the physical organs of the individual, whereas the continuum should be understood on the level of the subtle consciousness. So perhaps we could say that the substantial causes of consciousness are present in the form of a potential rather than as actual conscious states.

CONSCIOUSNESS

When we talk about consciousness, or *shes pa* in Tibetan, we are not talking about a single, unitary, monolithic entity that is 'out there'. We are referring, of course, to the mental consciousness which is the sixth consciousness according to Buddhist psychology.[7]

Generally speaking, when we try to investigate our mind through introspection, we find that it tends to be dominated either by discursive thoughts or by feelings and sensations. So let us try to examine how feelings and discursive thoughts occur within the mind.

Feelings, of course, can be considered in relation to two different dimensions of reality. We can speak about them purely at the physical level, as sensations, but when we try to understand feelings in terms of mental consciousness the issue is far more complex. And although we naturally accept that there must be connections between the consciousness and the nervous system of the body, we must somehow be able to account for deeper levels of feeling as well, or what we could call tones of experience.

I would like to point out that although very little research has been carried out in this area, and despite the fact that what little exists is still at a rudimentary stage, experiments done on meditators point to a phenomenon which may be difficult to account for within the current scientific paradigm. These experiments have shown that without any voluntary physical change in the body, and without any physical movement on the part of the individual, a person can affect his or her physiological state simply by using the power of the mind through a focused, single-pointed state. The physiological changes that take place are difficult to explain according to current assumptions about human physiology.

There is no doubt that our consciousness and all our experiences are contingent upon our body, so the human mind and the human body are in some sense inextricable. Yet at the same time, I feel that research seems to point to the possibility that the human mind also has a power of its own which can be enhanced through reflection and meditation, or training of the mind. Furthermore, it is well known that there is a growing recognition within modern medicine of the power of the will in the healing process. A person's willpower affects his physiology. How is willpower developed? It can be through thinking something through and discovering the reasonable grounds for one's understanding. It can also be through meditation. In whichever way it is developed, it is now acknowledged that the will can effect physical change.

What does this mean? What seems to be accepted scientifically is that all the thoughts that occur in our mind give rise to chemical changes and movements within the brain, which are then expressed in physiological change. But does pure thought lead to such physical effects too? And is it the case that thoughts occur solely as a result of chemical changes within the body or brain? I have asked scientists on several occasions whether it would be possible for the process to begin first with just pure thought, and then, secondly, thought processes occur which give rise to chemical changes, which in turn trigger physiological effects. Most of the time their answers have indicated that since it is assumed that consciousness is contingent upon a physical base (the brain, for instance), every occurrence of thought must necessarily be accompanied or caused by chemical changes in the brain. To me, however, that assumption seems to be based more on prejudice than experimental proof. I therefore think the question is still open and further research is needed, particularly involving practitioners who engage in profound meditation.

The Vajrayana literature contains discussions of the existence of different levels of consciousness, or different subtleties of mind, and the ways in which these correspond to subtle levels of energy. I think these explanations can contribute a great deal to our understanding of the nature of mind and its functions.

So, as we saw earlier, most of our conscious mind consists either of states related with objects that we have experienced in the past – recollections of past experiences inform our present consciousness – or it consists of some kind of feeling or sensation. As a result, it is very difficult for us to glimpse the actual nature of consciousness, which is the sheer state of knowing or the luminosity of mind. One technique that we can use in order to do this is sitting meditation, through which we free our mind from thoughts of past experiences and from any form of anticipation of the future. Instead, we abide in the nowness of the present, although we cannot really talk of a 'present' consciousness.

When you are able to clear away thoughts of the past and the future, slowly you begin to get a sense of the space between the two. You learn to abide in that present moment. In that space, you begin to glimpse what we call emptiness, and if you can remain in that emptiness for longer and longer periods of time then gradually the nature of consciousness itself, which is the sheer luminosity and natural awareness of mind, will slowly dawn in you. Through repeated practice this period can be lengthened more and more, so that your awareness of the nature of consciousness becomes clearer and clearer.

However, it is important to realize that this experience of the luminosity of mind, of the nature of mind, is not a profound realization in itself. Rebirth in many of the Formless Realms of samsara is considered to result from abiding in such states of clarity. On the other hand, if we know how to use that initial experience of luminosity as a basis, then we can build on it by complementing our meditation with other practices, and in this way it will become truly profound.

So here I have explained how we can look at the Buddha's teaching on the Truth of Suffering. Once you have developed this kind of recognition of the duhkha nature of life, you already have some understanding that at the root of our suffering lies a fundamental ignorance. This, of course, leads us to the Second Truth which is the Origin of Suffering.

Questions

Q: Your Holiness, if corporeal beings are impermanent due to their complex physical nature, are spiritual beings permanent because of their lack of physical substance?

HHDL: Let us take the example of a formless being, that is, a being who, according to Buddhism, is in the Formless Realm. Unlike beings in the Desire Realm or Form Realm, that sentient being may not be subject to the natural processes of decay to which corporeal beings are subject, yet it still remains impermanent because it has a limited lifespan during which it remains in the Formless Realm. Since its life there has a beginning and an end, it is still subject to the process of change.

However, if we are talking about a being who has attained the state of moksha and has become an arhat, then the situation is different. Similarly, bodhisattvas on very high levels of realization (from the eighth bodhisattva level onwards) are no longer subject to the process of ageing. In a sense one could say that from the point of view of the continuity of consciousness, there is a sense of permanence for such beings. Moreover, such beings are described in the scriptures as having a mental rather than a corporeal form. We should note that this mental form is very different from the 'mental body' that is described in Vajrayana, in relation to the after-death states, for example.

THREE

THE TRUTH OF THE ORIGIN OF SUFFERING

In the previous chapter we looked at the fact
that we all desire happiness and wish to overcome suffering, and how, despite this natural
aspiration, we tend to create the conditions
for more suffering because we do not know
the way to create the causes for happiness.
We found that at the root of this situation lies
a fundamental confusion or, in Buddhist
terminology, a fundamental ignorance. This
confusion applies not only to the way things
are but also to the way causes and effects
relate to each other. Therefore, in Buddhism
we talk about two types of ignorance, or
avidya: ignorance of the laws of causality,
specifically of the laws of karma, and ignorance of the ultimate nature of reality. These
relate respectively to the two levels of understanding of dependent origination that we

outlined in Chapter One. The first level was an understanding in terms of causal dependence, which dispels our ignorance of the laws of causality. The more profound level was an understanding in terms of the ultimate nature of reality, which dispels our fundamental ignorance.

However, this does not mean that ignorance is the only cause of our unenlightened existence. This has, of course, many other derivative causes and conditions, which are technically called *kleshas* or 'afflictive emotions and thoughts'. This is a very complex class of emotions and thoughts, described in detail in the Abhidharma literature. For example, according to Abhidharma there are six root afflictive emotions or thoughts, out of which arise 20 secondary types of emotions and thoughts. The Abhidharma therefore presents a comprehensive explanation of the whole world of thought and emotion.

There is another explanation of the process of being in samsara in the Tantric Vajrayana literature, which details the 80 types of thoughts or concepts which are indicative of our being in an unenlightened state. The

73

Kalachakra literature, which belongs to the Vajrayana class, further identifies the causes of samsaric existence in terms of propensities or natural dispositions.

These afflictive emotions and thoughts, which arise from our fundamental delusion, give rise to volitional actions. So together, delusions and karmic actions are the origins of our suffering.

Generally speaking, afflictive emotions and thoughts are defined as those of which the mere occurrence creates immediate disturbance within our mind. They then afflict us from within.

KARMA

Categories of Karmic Action

If that is the general definition of klesha, what is the definition of karma?[1] We should remember to situate karma within the context of the wider Buddhist understanding of the natural laws of causality. Karma is one particular instance of the natural causal laws that operate throughout the universe where, according to Buddhism, things and events come into being purely as a result of the combination of causes and conditions.

Karma, then, is an instance of the general law of causality. What makes karma unique is that it involves intentional action, and therefore an agent. The natural causal processes operating in the world cannot be termed karmic where there is no agent involved. In order for a causal process to be a karmic one, it must involve an individual whose intention would lead to a particular action. It is this specific type of causal mechanism which is known as karma.

So within the general field of karmic action we can talk about three different types of action which produce corresponding effects. Actions which produce suffering and pain are generally considered negative or non-virtuous actions. Actions that lead to positive and desirable consequences, such as experiences of joy and happiness, are considered to be positive or virtuous actions. The third category includes actions which lead to experiences of equanimity, or neutral feelings and experiences; these are considered to be neutral actions, and are neither virtuous nor non-virtuous.

In terms of the actual nature of karmic actions themselves, there are two principal types: mental acts – actions that are not necessarily manifested through physical action – and physical acts, which include both bodily and verbal acts. Then, from the point of view of the medium of expression of an action, we distinguish actions of the mind, of speech, and of the body. Furthermore, in the scriptures we also find discussions about karmic actions which are completely virtuous, completely non-virtuous, and those which are a mixture of the two. I feel that for many of us who practise the Dharma, most of our actions may be a mixture of the two.

If we analyse a single karmic action, we can see that there are several stages within that event. There is a beginning, which is the stage of the motivation or intention; there is the actual execution of the act; and then there is the culmination or completion of the act. According to the scriptures, the intensity and force of a karmic action vary according to the way each of these stages is carried out.

Let us take the example of a negative action. If, at the stage of motivation, the person has a very strong negative emotion like anger, and then acts on an impulse and carries out the action, but immediately afterwards feels deep regret for the action he has committed, all three stages would not be completely fulfilled. Consequently, the action would be less powerful compared to an instance where the person has acted out all stages completely – with a strong motivation, actual execution, and a sense of taking pleasure or satisfaction from the act committed. Similarly, there could be cases where the individual may have a very weak motivation but circumstances force him or her to actually commit the act. In this case, although a negative act has been committed it would be even less powerful than in our first example, because a strong motivating force was not present. So depending on the strength of the motivation, of the actual act, and of the completion, the karma produced will have corresponding degrees of intensity.

On the basis of these differences, the scriptures discuss four types of karma: karma which is carried out but not accumulated, karma which is accumulated but not carried out, karma where the act is both carried out and accumulated, and karma where there is an absence of both accumulation and the actual execution of the act. It is important to understand the significance of this point, and to appreciate that since there are different stages to every act, karmic actions themselves are composite, and their quality can be characterized as the cumulative result of each of their composing factors.

Once you appreciate this, then whenever you have the opportunity to engage in a positive action as a Dharma practitioner, it is important to ensure that at the initial stage your positive motivation is very strong, and that you have a strong intention to engage in the act. Then, while you are actually carrying out the act, you should ensure that you have given it your best, and you have put all your effort into making the action successful. Once the action is performed, it is important to ensure that you dedicate the positive karma that you have thereby created towards the well-being of all beings as well as your own attainment of enlightenment. If you can reinforce that dedication with an understanding of the ultimate nature of reality, it would be even more powerful.

Ideally, as Dharma practitioners, we should of course try to avoid engaging in any negative actions at all, but even if we do find ourselves in a situation where we are committing a non-virtuous action, it is impor-tant to make sure that at least our motivation is not strong and there is no strong emotion involved. Then, even while we are carrying out the action, if we have a strong pang of conscience, and a sense of regret or remorse, then of course the negative act will be very weak. Finally, the action should not be followed by any sense of satisfaction. We should not take pleasure in any negative action we have committed, but rather we should feel deep remorse and regret, and immediately afterwards we should purify the negativity, if possible. If we can do this, if we can live a way of life where we relate to our positive and negative actions in this way, then we will be able to follow the teachings on the law of karma much more effectively.

Although there are many different types of negative action, the Buddhist scriptures summarize them as the Ten Negative or Ten Non-virtuous Actions. There are three actions of body, four of speech, and three of mind. The three bodily negative actions are killing, stealing, and sexual misconduct; the four negative actions of speech are lying, engaging in divisive speech, using harsh words, and engaging in senseless gossip; and the three negative mental actions are covetousness, harbouring harmful thoughts and intentions, and holding wrong views. Ideally, a Dharma practitioner should live in such a way that he avoids all these negative actions if possible, and if not, then at least he should refrain from as many as he can. Leading a disciplined life and avoiding negative actions is what Buddhists understand as an ethical way of life.

Karma and the Person

How does a Buddhist practitioner actually go about trying to lead a moral life? A person's ultimate aspiration is to attain liberation from samsara, to attain spiritual freedom or enlightenment, so one of his or her principal tasks is to gain victory over the kleshas. However, there is no way that a practitioner can directly combat negative emotions and thoughts at the initial stage, so the sensible way to proceed is simply to find a way of containing the expression of the negative actions of our body, speech and mind. The first step, then, is to guard our body, speech and mind from engaging in negative actions so that we don't give in to the power and domination of our negative thoughts and emotions.

Once you have achieved this first stage, you can proceed to the second stage and tackle the root cause – the fundamental ignorance of which we spoke earlier. At this stage you are able to counteract the forces of the kleshas directly. Once you can do that, the third stage consists not simply of gaining victory over them, but also of rooting out all the propensities and imprints they have left within the psyche. This is why Aryadeva states in the *Four Hundred Verses on Madhyamaka* that a true spiritual aspirant must first overcome negative behaviour, in the middle phase must counter any grasping at self, and in the final stage should overcome all the views that bind us within the samsaric realm.[2]

As we have already seen, Buddhism explains how both the environment and the sentient beings living in that environment are produced as a result of fundamental ignorance, particularly the karma which arises from ignorance. However, we should not think that karma produces these things from out of nowhere. This is not the case. Karma is not like an eternal cause. We should realize that in order for karma to operate, and in order for it to have the potential to create its consequences, it must have a basis on which to do so. It follows that there exists a continuum of both the physical and the mental worlds. We can trace the continuum of the physical world to the beginning of a particular universe, and then we can even trace that 'beginning' to empty space. Buddhism accepts the existence of what are known as 'space particles' (namkhai dul), and asserts there is a stage of empty space in which the source of the material universe is in some sense contained. In the case of the mental world, we cannot say that the continuum of consciousness in sentient beings is a result of karma. Neither can we say that the unending process of the continuity of both matter and mind results from karma.

If this is the case, if the basic continuum is not produced by karma, then where does karma fit in? At what point does karma play a causal role in producing sentient beings and the natural environment in which they live? Perhaps we can say that there is a natural process in the world, and at a certain point when its evolution has reached a stage where it can affect the experiences of beings – giving rise to either painful experiences of suffering or joyful experiences of happiness – that is the point where karma enters the picture. After all, the karmic process only makes sense in relation to the experience of sentient beings.

So if we were to ask whether consciousness is produced by karma, or whether sentient beings are produced by karma, it seems the answer should be 'no'. But on the other hand, if we ask whether the human body and the human consciousness are products of karma, then the answer is 'yes' because both result from virtuous actions. This is because, when we talk about the human body and human consciousness, we are referring to a state of existence which is directly related to the painful and pleasurable experiences of an individual. Finally, if we were to ask whether or not our natural instinct to seek happiness and overcome suffering is a product of karma, it seems the answer would again be 'no'.

Karma and the Natural World

Now when we turn to the evolution of the physical universe at large, we cannot say that the natural processes of cause and effect are a product of karma. The process of cause and effect in the natural world takes place regardless of karma. Nevertheless, karma would have a role to play in determining the form that the process takes, or the direction in which it leads.

Here we should mention that from the Buddhist analytical point of view, we distinguish two realms of enquiry. One realm we could call 'natural', where only the natural process of causal laws operates, and the other is where certain properties emerge, contingent on these causal interactions. On account of this distinction we find that different avenues of reasoning are used when trying to understand the nature of the world or of reality.

For example, in Buddhist analysis we use what we call the Four Principles. The first is the *Principle of Nature*: the fact that things exist, and that causes lead to effects. We could almost say that this principle implies an acceptance of natural laws. Then we have the *Principle of Efficacy*: this deals with the way things have the capacity to produce certain results according to their nature. The third is the *Principle of Dependence*: given the first two principles, we see there is a natural dependence between things and events, between causes and effects. On the basis of these three principles, Buddhist critical analysis applies various types of reasoning to broaden or deepen our understanding of the natural world. Therefore the fourth principle we accept is the *Principle of Valid Proof*: given this, that must be the case; and given that, this should be the case.

For a practising Buddhist, it is important to appreciate these principles of the natural world, so that one is in a position to utilize that knowledge to live a life that is in accord with the principles of Dharma. We could therefore say that by living according to the Dharma we would be applying the Principle of Valid Proof, in terms of the way in which we avoid negative actions and enhance virtuous actions.

So, as I mentioned earlier, the questions we now have to consider are: at what point in the causal process does karma come into the picture? and in what manner does karma interact with the process of the natural causal laws?

Perhaps we can refer to our own personal experience in order to answer these questions. Experience shows that certain actions we do in the morning, for example, will have a continuing effect even in the evening. The action will have created a certain state of mind. It will have had an impact upon our emotion and our sense of being so even though it was committed in the morning as an event that is finished, its effect still lingers on in our mind. I think the same principle operates with karma and its effects, even in the case of long-term karmic effects. This is how we understand that karma can create effects which are felt even a long time after the act was committed. According to the Buddhist explanation, of course, the impact of karma can be felt over successive lifetimes as well as in our present life.

At this point I feel that unless we complement the general explanation of the karmic process found in the Buddhist literature[3] with points from the Vajrayana literature, our understanding will not be complete. The Vajrayana explains that both the physical world and the bodies of living beings are composed of the five elements: earth, water, fire, wind, and space. Space here should be understood in terms of vacuum, of empty space, rather than as space in the technical sense of absence of obstruction. The Vajrayana literature discusses these in terms of external elements and internal elements, and shows how they are related to each other at a very profound level. Through understanding this relationship, our insight into the way karma affects the world is a much deeper one.

As we discussed earlier, the fact that consciousness exists is a natural fact. Consciousness exists; that is it. Similarly, the continuum of consciousness is also a natural principle: consciousness maintains its continuity. To this we must add that in Buddhism, there is an understanding that consciousness cannot arise from nowhere or without a cause; and, at the same time, that consciousness cannot be produced from matter. This is not to say that matter cannot affect consciousness. However, the nature of consciousness is sheer luminosity, mere experience; it is the primordial knowing faculty, and therefore it cannot be produced from matter whose nature is different. It follows that since consciousness cannot arise without a cause, and since it cannot arise from a material cause, it must come from a ceaseless continuum. It is on this premise that Buddhism accepts the existence of (beginningless) former lives.[4]

We have seen that the origin of suffering lies in both karma and ignorance, but actually ignorance is the principal origin.

Karma and the Emotions

There are differences in the way each school of Buddhism understands the nature of the kleshas, corresponding to their various interpretations of the doctrine of *anatman*, or no-soul theory. For example, certain states of mind, and certain thoughts and emotions which, according to the Madhyamaka-Svatantrika and Chittamatra schools, may be considered non-delusory, are seen as delusory from the point of view of the Madhyamaka-Prasangika school. This is a very complex point, of course, and would require a lot of study.

The most important thing for us to know is that afflictive emotion is our ultimate enemy and a source of suffering. Once it develops within our mind, it immediately destroys our peace of mind, and eventually destroys our health, and even our friendships with other people. All negative activities such as killing, bullying, cheating and so forth, stem from afflictive emotion. This, therefore, is our real enemy.

An external enemy may be harmful to you today, but tomorrow could become very helpful, whereas the inner enemy is consistently destructive. Moreover, wherever you live the inner enemy is always there with you, and that makes it very dangerous. In contrast, we can often keep an external enemy at some kind of distance. In 1959, for example, we escaped from Tibet since escape was a physical possibility; but in the case of this inner enemy, whether I am in Tibet, or in the Potala, or in Dharamsala, or here in London, wherever I go it follows me. I think the inner enemy is even there in meditation; and even if I visualize a mandala, I may still find this enemy in its very centre! So this is the main point we have to realize: the real destroyer of our happiness is always there within us.

So what can we do about it? If it is not possible to work on that enemy and to eliminate it, then I think we had better forget the spiritual path and rely on alcohol and sex and other such things to improve our lives! However, if there is a possibility of eliminating the inner enemy, then I think we should take the opportunity of having a human body, a human brain and a good human heart, and combine these strengths to reduce and ultimately uproot it. This is why human life is considered to be so precious according to the Buddhist teachings, for it alone enables a being to train and transform the mind, mainly by virtue of intelligence and reasoning.

Buddhists distinguish between two kinds of emotion. One type is without reason, and is just based on prejudice. Hatred is one of these. This sort of emotion will rely on superficial reasons, of course, such as 'this person has hurt me terribly', but deep down, if you pursue that reasoning further, you find it does not go very far. Emotions without proper reason are what we call negative emotions. The other kind of emotion, which includes compassion and altruism, is emotion with reason because through deep investigation you can prove it is good, necessary and useful. Furthermore, although by nature it is a type of emotion, it is actually in accord with reason and intelligence. In fact, it is by combining our intelligence and emotion that we can change and transform our inner world.

So long as the inner enemy is there, and so long as we are under its control, there can be no permanent happiness. Understanding the need to defeat this enemy is true realization, and developing a keen desire to overcome it is the aspiration to seek freedom, technically called renunciation. Therefore this practice of analysing our emotions and our inner world is very crucial.

The scriptures say that so far as the desire to overcome the first level of suffering is concerned, the 'suffering of suffering', even animals have it naturally. And so far as the aspiration to free oneself from the second level of suffering is concerned, the 'suffering of change', this is not something that is unique to the Buddhist path. Many ancient Indian non-Buddhist paths were similar, seeking inner tranquillity through samadhi. However, the genuine aspiration to seek complete liberation from samsara can only arise from a recognition of the third level of suffering, the 'suffering of conditioning', where we realize that so long as we remain under the control of ignorance we will be subject to suffering, and there will be no room for lasting joy and happiness. It may be said that the recognition of this third level of suffering is unique to the Buddhist path.

QUESTIONS

Q: Could Your Holiness please explain why the result of karma is sometimes instant and why on other occasions we have to wait lifetimes before the causal effect occurs?

HHDL: One factor would be the intensity of the karmic action itself. Another factor is the extent to which the various other conditions that are necessary for that karma to ripen are complete, and this is dependent, in turn, on other karmic actions. Vasubandhu addressed this issue in the *Abhidharmakosha*, in which he states that, generally speaking, the karmic actions which are the most forceful tend to produce their effects first. If the intensity of a karmic action is equal to that of another karmic action, then the result of the action with which the individual is most familiar tends to ripen first. However if two karmic actions are equally forceful and equally familiar, then the one that is committed earlier tends to produce its result first.

Q: Is there a difference between thought and action with regard to karmic effects? In other words, can a thought cause an action and vice versa?

HHDL: As I explained, the Buddhist concept of karma is not confined to bodily action alone; it also embraces mental acts, or we could say emotional acts. For example, when we talk about an act of covetousness, or a harmful intention, these are not necessarily manifest in behaviour. One could think such thoughts fully and in detail without expressing them in action at all, so a certain completion of these acts does happen on the mental level.

Furthermore, there are certain types of actions which do not necessarily have an immediate motivation or intention, but because of the conditioning from past karmic actions, one could have a propensity to act in a certain way. This means that some actions can arise not as a result of motivation, but as a result of karmic tendencies.

THE TRUTH OF CESSATION

The third Noble Truth is the Truth of Cessation. The key questions we must ask ourselves on this are the following: What is nirvana? What is *moksha* or liberation? What do we mean by *nirodha* or cessation? And is it really possible to attain cessation or not?

If we were to reply that we must accept that liberation is possible on the grounds that Buddha spoke of it in the scriptures, I don't think that is a satisfactory answer. It may be useful to reflect on a point that Aryadeva makes in his *Four Hundred Verses on the Middle Way*. He argues that when we talk about the ultimate nature of reality, or emptiness, we must realize that the understanding of emptiness is not something which requires reliance on scriptural authority. We can approach it through critical analysis and reasoning.

In Buddhism, we assert that one category of phenomena manifest to us and can be perceived directly, so there is no need for any logical proof of their existence. A second category of phenomena may not be obvious to us, but we can infer their existence through a process of reasoning. These are technically known as 'slightly obscure phenomena'. Emptiness belongs to this second category.[1]

Since we can infer the truth of emptiness, we must also accept that liberation can be inferred through the reasoning process too. As Nagarjuna says, a true understanding of liberation should be based on an understanding of emptiness, because liberation is nothing other than the total elimination, or total cessation, of delusion and suffering through insight into emptiness. The concept of liberation is therefore very closely related to that of emptiness, and just as emptiness can be inferred, so can moksha.

On account of this intimate connection between emptiness and liberation in Buddhism, the passage in Maitreya's *Abhisamaya-lamkara* which deals with the third Noble Truth contains an extensive discussion of the

16 types of emptiness. The fact that liberation is an ultimate truth (and therefore related to emptiness) is explicitly discussed in Chandrakirti's writings as well. So it seems that our acceptance of liberation as a possibility is a function of how well we understand the concept of emptiness.

EMPTINESS

Four Interpretations of 'No-self' or Emptiness

When we talk about emptiness in Buddhism, it is clear that we are referring to the absence of something, a form of negation. In the same way, the no-self theory is a form of negation. Why such insistence on categorical negation? Once again, let us pause for a while and consider our experience.

Let's imagine that I have a certain fear based on some kind of suspicion that there might be something threatening nearby. If the thought occurs to me that I may be mistaken, that it may be my projection, then although it will lessen my fear it will not completely dispel it. However, if instead I develop the thought that it is pure and utter illusion, that there isn't anything there at all and I'm just imagining it, and if my negation is that categorical, then of course it will have an immediate impact on dispelling my fear. The question is: if that is the case, what is actually being negated? What is empty of what?

According to the scriptures, emptiness in this example is an absence of the object of negation, which in this case is the object of our fearful apprehension. This does not explain things fully, however, so we have to go further and try to understand what the object of negation actually is. The key to this question really lies in the way we understand the meaning of atman (self) in the context of anatman (no-self). Depending upon one's philosophical interpretation of the Buddha's teaching on anatman, there will be differences in the way one identifies what is being negated here.

Buddhist literature expresses varying degrees of subtlety concerning the identity of the atman as an object of negation. For instance, on one level[2] the atman is identified as substantially real, as a soul that exists within

each one of us, and so in this context anatman means the negation of a substantially
real, autonomous agent or eternal soul.

Then we have the interpretation of the
Chittamatra school, which understands fundamental ignorance not as the belief in a
substantially real and eternal soul, but rather
as the belief in the reality of the physical
world. The Chittamatrins understand fundamental ignorance, then, as the (erroneous)
belief in the duality of mind and matter, so
the object to be negated with respect to anatman is precisely this belief.

Thirdly, there is the Madhyamaka-Svatantrika understanding of emptiness. According to this school, although things come
into being as a result of causes and conditions, and although the status of things as
existing is in one sense or another dependent
on our perception, nevertheless there is a
certain intrinsic reality to things and events.
What is negated by this school is the asser-
tion that objects exist independent of perception, and it is this that constitutes their
understanding of emptiness.

From the point of view of the Madhyamaka-Prasangika school, however, that is not the final meaning of the Buddha's teaching on anatman. According to this view, so long as we have not deconstructed or dismantled the notion that things and events can have any type of intrinsic existence whatsoever, then we are still grasping at things as real, as though they enjoyed some kind of independent status. Therefore the Prasangika-Madhyamikas negate the intrinsic existence and identity of things and events, and claim that *this* is the true meaning of emptiness.

Despite these differences, what all four schools have in common is a concern to emphasize that while we are rightly engaged in counteracting our grasping at the self, it is important to ensure that our negation does not defy the reality of the conventional world, the world of lived experience. There is a shared understanding that causality and the operation of karma should not be negated in the process. It seems that the Madhyamaka-Prasangika approach is the most successful in this respect, in so far as it uses a form of analysis that allows a thorough and complete negation of atman, while at the same time ensuring that the world of dependent origination and of karma is not destroyed but, on the contrary, re-affirmed.

The Middle Way

There is a very important passage[1] in Nagarjuna's *Fundamental Treatise on the Middle Way* (*Madhyamakamulakarika*), where he states: 'That which is dependently originated, I call empty. And that is, in turn, dependently designated.' The idea is that whatever is dependently originated is empty in the ultimate sense, and that what we designate, dependently, is nothing other than empty phenomena. The fact that things and events are dependently designated implies that they are not non-existent, they are not mere nothingness. So when an understanding of dependent origination is combined with an understanding of emptiness, we find that this enables an individual to tread the Middle Way, so-called because it avoids the extremes of absolutism and nihilism.

So the Madhyamaka expression 'dependently designated' has a deep significance. The first word, 'dependently', implies that things and events come into being through dependence on other factors, which means that they do not possess independent, autonomous, or absolute existence. So this first point negates absolutism. The second word, 'designated', implies that things and events are not mere nothingness, that they are not non-existent – that they do indeed exist. This part of the expression therefore ensures that the reality of the phenomenal world is not denied. As Buddhapalita states in his commentary on the *Fundamentals of the Middle Way*, if things and events have an independent existential status, and come into being without depending on other factors, then why are their designations dependent and interrelated?

In connection with this point, I have been told by various physicists that they are beginning to have problems in postulating an idea of reality that is in accordance with the quantum understanding of the physical world – even as a concept, reality is a problem. For me, this points to the difficulty of finding essences when we look into the essence of things. However, if we jump to the other extreme and say that everything is pure illusion and a mere projection of the mind, then we will be falling into the trap into which the Chittamatrins fell, namely the view of total mentalism. So if things do not possess intrinsic reality and yet, at the same time, if we are not happy with the conclusion that everything is a mere projection of the mind, what is the alternative? What is the middle way? The answer given by the Madhyamikas is that things and events arise purely as a result of the aggregation of many factors, and their conventional existence stems from the identity we impute to each aggregation.

As regards the exposition of the Buddhist doctrine of emptiness generally, we find there are many forms of reasoning presented in the literature which are designed to lead to an understanding of emptiness. Of all of these, the reasoning that is based on the understanding of dependent origination is considered to be the most effective. In order to develop the most profound understanding of the meaning of dependent origination, I think the works of Buddhapalita and Chandrakirti are crucial. Much of my own understanding and, naturally, most of the presentation I am making here, is based on Lama Tsongkhapa's exposition of these topics, which in turn is very much based on the reading of Nagarjuna by Chandrakirti and Buddhapalita, to the extent that Tsongkhapa substantiates almost every crucial point by referring to the commentaries of these two great masters.

When I study Nagarjuna's *Fundamentals of the Middle Way*, I combine the 23rd chapter dealing with the 12 links of dependent origination, with the 18th chapter on anatman. This latter chapter shows how it is the process of grasping at an eternal principle, or a substantially real soul, that binds us to unenlightened existence. It further shows how negating the principle of atman, and eliminating that grasping, lead to liberation. The main point is to underline how important it is to gain insight into emptiness.

I then combine my study of these two chapters with that of the 24th, in which Nagarjuna anticipates a number of the objections which could be put forward by the realist schools of Buddhism. The core of their objections could be summarized in this way: if there is no intrinsic reality, and if there is no intrinsic existence and identity to things and events, then there is no-thing. It follows that there cannot be any Four Noble Truths; if there are no Four Noble Truths there are no Three Jewels; if there are no Three Jewels there cannot be a Path to enlightenment. Nagarjuna responds by turning the realists' own criticism against them by saying that, on the contrary, if things do exist intrinsically then the consequences the realists attribute to his argument would apply to theirs. That is to say, if things are intrinsically real then the Four Noble Truths would not apply, nor could causes produce effects. So the central message of that chapter is to demonstrate that what Nagarjuna means by emptiness is not a mere nothingness, or a mere non-existence. Emptiness should be understood in terms of the interdependent nature of reality: it is by virtue of their dependent origination that things are devoid of independent existence.

Lodrö Gyatso, a Tibetan master from Amdo, captured this point in a beautiful verse.[4] He said that emptiness in this context does not mean the absence of functionality. What does it mean then? It is the emptiness of real or absolute existence. Dependent origination does not entail intrinsic reality or intrinsic identity, but what it does entail is illusion-like, phenomenal reality. So when you understand the meaning of both emptiness and dependent origination, you can posit emptiness and appearance simultaneously, within one locus, without contradiction.

Furthermore, the same master added that all philosophical schools describe their own position as avoiding the extreme of absolutism by talking about some form of emptiness, and avoiding the other extreme of nihilism by talking about the level of phenomenal reality. He pointed out, however, that it is only when you reverse the process that you overcome all forms of clinging: that is the Madhyamaka-Prasangika position, of course. From the point of view of Madhyamaka-Prasangika, then, it is through understanding appearance that a person is liberated from

grasping onto absolutes, and it is by understanding the true meaning of emptiness that a
person is freed from falling into nihilism.

The Madhyamaka Schools

Earlier I spoke about there being two different
understandings of emptiness even within the
Madhyamaka school itself, and I outlined
how the Madhyamaka-Svatantrika view differs
from that of the Madhyamaka-Prasangika.
The basis for accepting this difference comes
from the writings of Bhavaviveka, one of the
chief disciples of Nagarjuna, who subjects the
Buddhist realist schools to very critical examination, and at the same time criticizes
Buddhapalita's reading of Nagarjuna. Bhavaviveka's own position emerges through these
two critiques. In essence, he maintains that
although they deny absolute existence, they
do accept some form of intrinsic and objective reality to things and events, which
Madhyamaka-Prasangika masters like Chandrakirti totally reject. So although Chandrakirti, Buddhapalita and Bhavaviveka were
all great disciples of Nagarjuna, there is a

substantial difference in their respective understanding of Nagarjuna's philosophy of emptiness. It is on account of this difference that Tibetan Buddhist scholars distinguish two divisions within the Madhyamaka school, which they call Svatantrika and Prasangika.

These two schools also differ in their methodology. The Madhyamaka-Prasangikas lay much greater emphasis on what is called the consequentialist style of reasoning. This resembles the *reductio ad absurdum* where you are not so much using reason to affirm something yourself, but rather you are concerned with showing the internal inconsistencies of your opponent's standpoint. In contrast, the Madhyamaka-Svatantrikas tend to use a syllogistic type of reasoning to establish their own positions.

Furthermore, there is another fundamental difference between Bhavaviveka and Chandrakirti which concerns the way our senses perceive material objects. For Bhavaviveka, it is valid to say that when a visual perception arises we see the appearance of an objective entity, because he accepts that things do possess a degree of objectivity which is then projected on to the perception. This is totally rejected by the Madhyamaka-Prasaṅgika school of Chandrakirti. It is clear, therefore, that the central point of difference between the two Madhyamaka schools is whether or not one accepts any idea of intrinsicality.

Applying our Understanding of Emptiness

The reason why it is so important to understand this subtle point is because of its implications for interpreting our own personal experience of life. When strong emotions arise in you, say attachment or anger, if you examine the experience of that emotion you will see that underlying it is an assumption that there is something objective and real out there which you are holding on to, and on to which you project desirable or undesirable qualities. According to the kind of qualities you project on to a thing or event, you feel either attracted to it or repulsed by it. So strong emotional responses in fact assume the existence of some form of objective reality.

However, if you realize that there is no intrinsic reality to things and events then, of course, this will automatically help you to understand that no matter how real and strong emotions may seem, they have no valid basis. Once you know that they are actually based on a fundamental misconception of reality, then the emotions themselves become untenable. On the other hand, if your understanding of emptiness is not thorough, in the sense that you have not succeeded in negating the notion of intrinsicality completely, then of course your attitude towards emotion will be somewhat ambivalent, and you may feel that there is some sense in which it is valid or justified.

When you have developed a certain understanding of emptiness, albeit an intellectual one, you will have a new outlook on things and events which you can compare to your usual responses. You will notice how much we tend to project qualities on to the world. More especially, you will realise that most of our strong emotions arise from assuming the reality of something that is unreal. In this way you may be able to gain an experiential sense of the disparity between the way you perceive things and the way things really are.

The moral that we can draw from all of this is that the strong emotions which afflict our mind arise from a fundamental state of confusion, which leads us to apprehend things as real and existing independently. In conclusion, we know that afflictive emotions and thoughts have no valid basis, neither in our experience, nor in reality, nor in reason.

By contrast, your insight into the emptiness of things is not only grounded in reason but also in experience: it has valid support. In addition, your understanding of emptiness and your grasping at things as real are directly opposed to one other, so one cancels the other out. Since they are opposing forces, and given that one has valid grounding whereas the other does not, the final conclusion we can draw is that the more we deepen our understanding of emptiness, and the greater the power of our insight becomes, the more we see through the deception of emotions, and consequently the weaker those emotions become. Indeed, we come to realize that strong afflictive emotions and thoughts, and their basis which is ignorance, can be weakened, while insight into emptiness can be enhanced.

LIBERATION

We have arrived at a point in our examination where we can conceivably accept that the power of delusions and of ignorance can be reduced, but the question remains as to whether it is at all possible to eliminate them completely and eradicate them from our minds. Some of the points in Maitreya's *Uttaratantra* may be very critical here. According to that text, our potential for knowledge is intrinsic to our consciousness and is an inherent, natural quality of our mind, whereas all those factors which afflict the mind are not an essential part of it. Mental afflictions are distinct from the essential nature of our mind, and are therefore called adventitious.

So when we talk about gaining the perfect wisdom of a buddha, we should not think that we need to create qualities in ourselves that are not there already, and acquire them from somewhere outside of us. Rather, we should see perfect buddha wisdom as a potential that is being realized. The defilements of the mind hamper the natural expression of that potential which is inherent in our consciousness. It is as if the capacity for unobstructed knowledge is there in our mind, but the defilements obscure and hinder it from being fully developed and expressed. However, once our understanding of the mind is informed by the idea that the essential nature of mind is pure luminosity and mere experience, or the sheer capacity to know, we can then conceive of the possibility of eliminating these afflictions completely.

To sum up, in this chapter we have followed the conceptual approach to the question of whether or not it is actually possible to attain liberation.

Finally, if we accept that liberation is possible, how exactly is it to be understood? In the scriptures, liberation is characterized in terms of four features. The first feature describes it as the true cessation of the continuum of afflictions. According to the second feature, liberation is true peace, the state of total tranquillity where the individual has attained complete freedom from all defilements of the mind. It is described in the third feature as totally satisfying, because one has reached ultimate satisfaction. Fourthly, it is described as definite emergence, in the sense that one has definitely emerged from the process of unenlightened existence.

FIVE

THE TRUTH OF THE PATH

If we accept that liberation is an achievable goal, how is it possible to achieve it? This question brings us to the fourth Noble Truth, which deals with the true path.

According to the Madhyamaka explanation, the true path should be understood in terms of developing a direct intuitive realization of emptiness. This is because the intuitive realization of emptiness leads directly to the attainment of cessation. However, in order to have such a realization one must have a basis in single-pointed meditation, since this is what leads to an experiential knowledge of emptiness. The point at which an individual attains that experiential knowledge[1] is said to be the beginning of what is called the Path of Connection or Path of Preparation, and the point at which he gains direct intuitive realization of emptiness is called the Path of Seeing.

The experiential knowledge of emptiness must in turn be based on an intellectual understanding of emptiness, developed through inference. Indeed, without that, it is impossible to attain a meditatively-based experience of emptiness. That initial stage of developing intellectual understanding is part of what is known as the Path of Accumulation. The threshold of this path is the point where the practitioner develops a genuine aspiration to attain liberation – and this we consider to be the very beginning of the Buddhist Path.

The Shravakayana Path

Even before we embark upon the Path,[2] a great deal of preparation is necessary. To begin with, the most important practice is that of the three higher trainings: the trainings in morality (Skt. shila), concentration or meditation (Skt. samadhi), and wisdom or insight (Skt. prajña). The scriptures generally describe the transition from one stage to another in terms of a meditator's experience.

It is important to understand, therefore, that the actual path on which the individual travels is that of his or her progressively deepening knowledge and realization of emptiness, technically known as the wisdom aspect of the path. Moreover, the wisdom that realizes emptiness must be developed within the context of the union of the single-pointedness of mind and penetrative insight, known as the union of shamatha and vipashyana.

In order to experience a union of these two, we have to develop shamatha first, for only this will enable us to channel our energy and concentration. Training in shamatha is therefore key. For it to be successful two factors must be present, namely the application of mindfulness and the application of mental alertness. These two capacities themselves will only develop successfully if our single-pointedness of mind is based on an ethically sound life, in which we apply discipline both to our attitude and to our way of life. This, of course, underlines the fundamental importance of morality. So now we can see how the three trainings are connected to each other.

All of these practices are common to both the Shravakayana and the Mahayana.

The Mahayana Path

We must now look at another important aspect of Buddhism, namely the way that the entire teaching of Buddha is founded on compassion. Compassion is the very foundation of the Dharma. The practice of enhancing our good heart and developing an altruistic mind is aimed at deepening our understanding of compassion, and invigorating the compassionate potential that exists within us. It is on the basis of profound compassion that we develop the altruistic aspiration to seek enlightenment for the benefit of all.

Traditionally this is called the generation of bodhichitta. What is bodhichitta? In Maitreya's *Abhisamayalamkara* bodhichitta is described as having two motivating factors: the first is genuine compassion towards all beings, and the second is recognition of the need to attain full enlightenment in order to fulfil the welfare of others. Indeed, to develop the altruistic mind of bodhichitta, it is not enough to have mere compassion. Bodhichitta must be based on a compassion which carries a sense of responsibility so that you are willing to take upon yourself the task of helping others.

This sense of responsibility will only arise if you have generated a spontaneous, genuine compassion which extends to all sentient beings without exception. This is universal compassion. It is called *mahakaruna* or 'great compassion' to distinguish it from ordinary compassion which is limited. However, this itself will not arise unless you have genuine insight into the nature of suffering, both your own suffering and that of others. You recognize your state as being one of suffering, then you will also feel a genuine empathy and connection with others. So far as gaining insight into the nature of suffering is concerned, reflection on the first Noble Truth, the Truth of Suffering, will assist you in deepening your insight.

For an altruistic practitioner, it is important to realize that attaining liberation for oneself alone is not enough. Not only is it individualistic, but even from the point of view of one's own path to perfection, it is not a state of full awakening.

It is therefore crucial to nurture our natural empathy and our sense of closeness with others. One of the methods described in the Buddhist scriptures for doing this is to imagine that all beings are your mothers, or someone else who is dear to you. You awaken the compassion you naturally feel for your mother or someone dear, and extend it to all other beings. In this way you develop a natural and spontaneous empathy. However, empathy cannot arise if your emotions towards others fluctuate due to the fact that you view some as enemies and others as friends. That discrimination has to be overcome first, and for this the practice of equanimity is fundamental.

A different method is presented by Shantideva in *The Guide to the Bodhisattva's Way of Life* (*Bodhicharyavatara*). He explains a way of cultivating genuine empathy by considering others as equal to oneself. For example, just as you personally wish to be happy and overcome suffering, others too have a similar desire, and just as you have the right to achieve this, so do they. With that sense of equality you reverse your self-centred perspective, putting yourself in others' shoes and relating to them as if they were dearer to you than you are to yourself.

According to the Tibetan tradition, these two different methods are combined and then meditated upon. Once you have gained even a simulated experience of the altruistic mind as a result of your reflection and meditation, then the custom is to stabilize and reinforce it by participating in a ceremony where you explicitly generate bodhichitta. This should then be followed by a keen desire to engage in the activities of a bodhisattva. According to tradition, the practitioner formally takes the vows of a bodhisattva at that point. The bodhisattva ideal, or the activities of a bodhisattva, are summed up in the Three Precepts: the first is the precept of refraining from negative actions; the second is the precept of deliberately engaging in virtuous actions; and the third is the precept of helping others.

From the point of view of how causal practices lead to a resultant state, bodhisattva practices are also sometimes described in terms of the two accumulations: the accumulations of merit and wisdom. The two accumulations come together in the union of method and wisdom and, in the Buddhist path, should never be separated.

The Vajrayana Path

The profundity and sophistication of Tantra or Vajrayana stem from the practice of unifying method and wisdom. To put it very briefly, one of the unique features of the union of method and wisdom in the Vajrayana teachings is that the practitioner first subjects his or her perception of self and the world to an understanding of emptiness, and dissolves everything into emptiness. That cognition of emptiness is then visualized (imaginatively, of course, at the beginning) as the perfect form of a meditational deity. Next, you reflect on the non-substantial or empty nature of that deity. So within one instance of cognition, both method and wisdom are present and complete: there is visualization of a deity and at the same time an understanding of the empty nature of that deity.

Within the Vajrayana tradition there are four principal classes of tantra according to the Gelug, Sakya and Kagyu schools; these are Kriya tantra, Carya tantra, Yoga tantra, and Highest Yoga tantra (Anuttarayogatantra). The first two classes do not involve taking Vajrayana vows; it is in the Yoga tantra and Highest Yoga tantra that tantric vows are taken. The Highest Yoga tantra also has meditative practices which use various physiological elements, such as visualizing the energy channels of the body, the energies that flow within the channels, the 'subtle drops', and so on. In all of these various types of meditation the key is always the aspiration of bodhichitta and insight into emptiness. Without these two factors none of them would even be considered to be Buddhist practices.

However, in some very reliable and authentic texts belonging to Yoga tantra, it is said that the Vajrayana path can also be based on the understanding of emptiness held by the Chittamatra school, not necessarily on that of the Madhyamaka. Despite this, I feel that if tantric practice is to be comprehensive, and if one is to attain full realization of the tantric path, an insight into emptiness based on the Madhyamaka is actually crucial.

Advice on Following the Buddhist Path

There are three pieces of advice I would like to share with you.

The first is to say that unless you are able to establish a firm grounding in the basic practices of the Buddha Dharma, such as those I have outlined, then even the supposedly profound practices of the Vajrayana will have no effect. The point is that for a practising Buddhist, it is really vital to develop an understanding of the Four Noble Truths, and to meditate upon them. Meditation should therefore be an essential part of your practice, and include both shamatha and vipashyana.

Another important factor is your determination. You should not imagine that all these developments can take place within a few days or a few years; they may even take several aeons, so determination is evidently vital. If you consider yourself a Buddhist and want to really practise Buddha Dharma, then right from the start you must make up your mind to do so until the end, regardless of whether it takes millions or billions of aeons. After all, what is the meaning of our life? In itself, there is no intrinsic meaning. However, if we use life in a positive way, then even the days and the months and the aeons can become meaningful. On the other hand, if you just fritter your life away aimlessly then even one day feels too long. You will find that once you have a firm determination and a clear objective, then time is not important.

As Shantideva writes in this beautiful prayer:

> For as long as space exists
> And sentient beings endure,
> May I too remain,
> To dispel the misery of the world.[3]

His words really convey a certain understanding to me, and they are so inspiring.

My final point is that the more impatient you are, and the more you want the way that is quickest, cheapest or best, the more likely you are to obtain a poor result. So I suggest this is the wrong approach.

CONCLUSION

If I were to essentialize my talk, I would say that if your understanding of the Four Noble Truths arises from deep reflections such as these, then you will gain a profound admiration for the Dharma, which is the true Refuge, and you will also develop a conviction in the possibility of actualizing the Dharma within yourself. On the basis of such a conviction you will be able to develop genuine devotion in the Buddha, the master who showed you the path, and you will also have a deep respect for the Sangha members who are your spiritual companions on the path.

If your understanding of the Three Jewels is based on a realization of the Four Noble Truths that is as profound as this, then whenever you think of Buddha, Dharma, and Sangha, they will come alive for you with renewed freshness. This is what is meant by Going for Refuge.

In fact, to summarize even more succinctly, the whole of the explanation I have given here is to show what is meant by Going for Refuge in the Three Jewels.

Although my own practice is very poor, very poor indeed, and although I recite mantras and visualize certain mandalas, even so the main emphasis of my daily practice is the Four Noble Truths and bodhichitta. These two practices I feel are of real practical benefit. Sometimes I think that visualizing deities can almost be like a way of deceiving oneself. In my view we must pursue practice step-by-step, with patience and determination. If you practise in this way, then after a year or after a decade you will notice at least some improvement in yourself, and when you see that, it brings a new encouragement to continue. However, we must realize that change is not at all easy.

So now you have read these teachings on the Four Noble Truths, if you consider you are a Buddhist then please put them into practice. They should not remain merely on an intellectual level. Practice and teaching must be part of our life. The same applies, of course, to practitioners and believers of other faiths, such as Christians, Muslims or Jews: whatever your faith, if you accept that faith then it must become part of your life. It is not sufficient to attend church on Sunday and join your hands together in prayer for a few moments, if the rest of your behaviour remains the same. Whether or not you are physically in a church or a cathedral, I think the teaching of your own religion must be in your heart. That's very important. Only then will you have an experience of it that is of real value, otherwise it is simply a piece of knowledge in your head and when you are faced with problems in life it won't be of any help.

Once the teaching is part of your life, whenever you have a real problem it gives you inner strength. Also, when you grow old, or have an incurable illness, and when death finally comes, then your practice truly gives you some kind of inner guarantee. After all, death is part of life; there is nothing strange about it; sooner or later we all have to pass through that gate. At that time, whether or not there is a life after, it is very valuable to have peace of mind. How can we achieve peace of mind at such a moment? It is possible only if we have some experience in ourselves that will provide inner strength, because no-one else can provide this for us – no deities, no gurus, and no friends. This is why the Buddha says you must be your own master.

COMPASSION, THE BASIS
FOR HUMAN HAPPINESS

Public talk given by His Holiness the Dalai Lama in the Free Trade Hall, Manchester, UK 19th July 1996

I think that every human being has an innate sense of 'I'. We cannot explain why that feeling is there, but it is. Along with it comes a desire for happiness and a wish to overcome suffering. This is quite justified: we have a natural right to achieve as much happiness as possible, and we also have the right to overcome suffering.

The whole of human history has developed on the basis of this feeling. In fact it is not limited to human beings; from the Buddhist point of view, even the tiniest insect has this feeling and, according to its capacity, is trying to gain some happiness and avoid unhappy situations.

However, there are some major differences between human beings and other animal species. They stem from human intelligence. On account of our intelligence, we are much more advanced and have a greater capacity. We are able to think much further into the future, and our memory is powerful enough to take us back many years. Furthermore, we have oral and written traditions which remind us of events many centuries ago. Now, thanks to scientific methods, we can even examine events which occurred millions of years ago.

So our intelligence makes us very smart, but at the same time, precisely because of that fact, we also have more doubts and suspicions, and hence more fears. I think the imagination of fear is much more developed in humans than in other animals. In addition, the many conflicts within the human family and within one's own family, not to mention the conflicts within the community and between nations, as well as the internal conflicts within the individual – all conflicts and contradictions arise from the different ideas and views our intelligence brings. So unfortunately, intelligence can sometimes create a quite unhappy state of mind. In this sense, it becomes another source of human misery. Yet, at the same time, I think that ultimately intelligence is the tool with which we can overcome all these conflicts and differences.

From this point of view, of all the various species of animal on the planet, human beings are the biggest troublemakers. That is clear. I imagine that if there were no longer any humans on the planet, the planet itself would be safer! Certainly millions of fish, chicken and other small animals might enjoy some sort of genuine liberation!

It is therefore important that human intelligence be utilized in a constructive way. That is the key. If we utilize its capacity properly, then not only human beings would become less harmful to each other, and to the planet, but also individual human beings would be happier in themselves. It is in our hands. Whether we utilize our intelligence in the right way or the wrong way is up to us. Nobody can impose their values on us. How can we learn to use our capacity constructively? First, we need to recognize our nature and then, if we have the determination, there is a real possibility of transforming the human heart.

On this basis, I will speak today on how a human being can find happiness as an individual, because I believe the individual is the key to all the rest. For change to happen in any community, the initiative must come from the individual. If the individual can become a good, calm, peaceful person, this automatically brings a positive atmosphere to the family around him or her. When parents are warm-hearted, peaceful and calm people, generally speaking their children will also develop that attitude and behaviour.

The way our attitude works is such that it is often troubled by outside factors, so one side of the issue is to eliminate the existence of trouble around you. The environment, meaning the surrounding situation, is a very important factor for establishing a happy frame of mind. However, even more important is the other side of the issue, which is one's own mental attitude.

The surrounding situation may not be so friendly, it may even be hostile, but if your inner mental attitude is right, then the situation will not disturb your inner peace. On the other hand, if your attitude is not right, then even if you are surrounded by good friends and the best facilities, you cannot be happy. This is why mental attitude is more important than external conditions. Despite this, it seems to me that many people are more concerned about their external conditions, and neglect the inner attitude of mind. I suggest that we should pay more attention to our inner qualities.

There are a number of qualities which are important for mental peace, but from the little experience I have, I believe that one of the most important factors is human compassion and affection: a sense of caring.

Let me explain what we mean by compassion. Usually, our concept of compassion or love refers to the feeling of closeness we have with our friends and loved ones. Sometimes compassion also carries a sense of pity. This is wrong – any love or compassion which entails looking down on the other is not genuine compassion. To be genuine, compassion must be based on respect for the other, and on the realization that others have the right to be happy and overcome suffering just as much as you. On this basis, since you can see that others are suffering, you develop a genuine sense of concern for them.

As for the closeness we feel towards our friends, this is usually more like attachment than compassion. Genuine compassion should be unbiased. If we only feel close to our friends, and not to our enemies, or to the countless people who are unknown to us personally and towards whom we are indifferent, then our compassion is only partial or biased.

As I mentioned before, genuine compassion is based on the recognition that others have the right to happiness just like yourself, and therefore even your enemy is a human being with the same wish for happiness as you, and the same right to happiness as you. A sense of concern developed on this basis is what we call compassion; it extends to everyone, irrespective of whether the person's attitude towards you is hostile or friendly.

One aspect of this kind of compassion is a sense of caring responsibility. When we develop that kind of motivation, our self-confidence increases automatically. This in turn reduces fear, and that serves as a basis for determination. If you are really determined right from the beginning to accomplish a difficult task, then even if you fail first time, second time, third time, it doesn't matter. Your aim is very clear, so you will continue to make an effort. This sort of optimistic and determined attitude is a key factor for success.

Compassion also brings us an inner strength. Once it is developed, it naturally opens an inner door, through which we can communicate with fellow human beings, and even other sentient beings, with ease, and heart to heart. On the other hand, if you feel hatred and ill-feeling towards others, they may feel similarly towards you, and as a result suspicion and fear will create a distance between you and make communication difficult. You will then feel lonely and isolated. Not all members of your community will have similar negative feelings towards you, but some may look on you negatively because of your own feeling.

If you harbour negative feelings towards others, and yet expect them to be friendly to you, you are being illogical. If you want the atmosphere around you to be more friendly, you must first create the basis for that. Whether the response of others is positive or negative, you must first create the ground of friendliness. If others still respond to you negatively after this, then you have the right to act accordingly.

I always try to create a ground of friendliness with people. Whenever I meet someone new, for example, I feel no need for introductions. The person is obviously another human being. Maybe sometime in the future, technological advances may mean that I could confuse a robot for a human being, but up to now this has never happened. I see a smile, some teeth and eyes, and so on, and I recognize the person as a human being! On that basis, on the emotional level we are the same, and basically on the physical level we are the same, except for colouring. But whether Westerners have yellow hair, or blue hair, or white hair, does not really matter. The important thing is that we are the same on the emotional level. With that conviction, I feel that the other person is a human brother, and approach him spontaneously. In most cases, the other person immediately responds accordingly, and becomes a friend. Sometimes I fail, and then I have the liberty to react according to the circumstances.

Basically, therefore, we should approach others openly, recognizing each person as another human being just like ourselves. There is not so much difference between us all.

Compassion naturally creates a positive atmosphere, and as a result you feel peaceful and content. Wherever there lives a compassionate person, there is always a pleasant atmosphere. Even dogs and birds approach the person easily. Almost fifty years ago, I used to keep some birds in the Norbulingka Summer Palace, in Lhasa. Among them was a small parrot. At that time I had an elderly attendant whose appearance was somewhat unfriendly – he had very round, stern eyes – but he was always feeding this parrot with nuts and so on. So whenever the attendant would appear, just the sound of his footsteps or his coughing would mean the parrot would show some excitement. The attendant had an extraordinarily friendly manner with that small bird, and the parrot also had an amazing response to him. On a few occasions I fed him some nuts but he never showed such friendliness to me, so I started to poke him with a stick, hoping he might react differently; the result was totally negative. I was using more force than the bird had, so it reacted accordingly.

Therefore, if you want a genuine friend, first you must create a positive atmosphere around you. We are social animals, after all, and friends are very important. How can you bring a smile to people's faces? If you remain stony and suspicious, it is very difficult. Perhaps if you have power or money, some people may offer you an artificial smile, but a genuine smile will only come from compassion.

The question is how to develop compassion. In fact, can we really develop unbiased compassion at all? My answer is that we definitely can. I believe that human nature is gentle and compassionate, although many people, in the past and now, think that it is basically aggressive. Let us examine this point.

At the time of conception, and while we are in our mother's womb, our mother's compassionate and peaceful mental state is a very positive factor for our development. If the mother's mind is very agitated, it is harmful for us. And that is just the beginning of life! Even the parents' state of mind at conception is important. If a child is conceived through rape, for example, then it will be unwanted, which is a terrible thing. For conception to take place properly, it should come from genuine love and mutual respect, not just mad passion. It is not enough to have some casual love affair, the two partners should know each other well and respect each other as people; this is the basis for a happy marriage. Furthermore, marriage itself should be for life, or at least should be long lasting. Life should properly start from such a situation.

Then, according to medical science, in the few weeks after birth, the child's brain is still growing. During that period, the experts claim that physical touch is a crucial factor for the proper development of the brain. This alone shows that the mere growth of our body requires another's affection.

After birth, one of the first acts on the mother's side is to give milk, and from the child's side it is to suckle. Milk is often considered a symbol of compassion. Without it, traditionally the child cannot survive. Through the process of suckling there comes a closeness between mother and child. If that closeness is not there, then the child will not seek its mother's breast, and if the mother is feeling dislike towards the child her milk may not come freely. So milk comes with affection. This means that the first act of our life, that of taking milk, is a symbol of affection. I am always reminded of this when I visit a church and see Mary carrying Jesus as a small baby; that to me is a symbol of love and affection.

It has been found that those children who grow up in homes where there is love and affection have a healthier physical development and study better at school. Conversely, those who lack human affection have more difficulty in developing physically and mentally. These children also find it difficult to show affection when they grow up, which is such a great tragedy.

Now let us look at the last moment of our lives – death. Even at the time of death, although the dying person can no longer benefit much from his friends, if he is surrounded by friends his mind may be more calm. Therefore throughout our lives, from the very beginning right up to our death, human affection plays a very important role.

An affectionate disposition not only makes the mind more peaceful and calm, but it affects our body in a positive way too. On the other hand, hatred, jealousy and fear upset our peace of mind, make us agitated and affect our body adversely. Even our body needs peace of mind, and is not suited to agitation. This shows that an appreciation of peace of mind is in our blood.

Therefore, although some may disagree, I feel that although the aggressive side of our nature is part of life, the dominant force of life is human affection. This is why it is possible to strengthen that basic goodness which is our human nature.

We can also approach the importance of compassion through intelligent reasoning. If I help another person, and show concern for him or her, then I myself will benefit from that. However, if I harm others, eventually I will be in trouble. I often joke, half sincerely and half seriously, saying that if we wish to be truly selfish then we should be wisely selfish rather than foolishly selfish. Our intelligence can help to adjust our attitude in this respect. If we use it well, we can gain insight as to how we can fulfil our own self-interest by leading a compassionate way of life. It would even be possible to argue that being compassionate is ultimately selfish.

In this context, I do not think that selfishness is wrong. Loving oneself is crucial. If we do not love ourselves, how can we love others? It seems that when some people talk of compassion, they have the notion that it entails a total disregard for one's own interests – a sacrificing of one's interests. This is not the case. In fact genuine love should first be directed at oneself.

There are two different senses of self. One has no hesitation in harming other people, and that is negative and leads to trouble. The other is based on determination, will-power and self-confidence, and that sense of 'I' is very necessary. Without it, how can we develop the confidence we need to carry out any task in life? Similarly, there are two types of desire also. However, hatred is invariably negative and destructive of harmony.

How can we reduce hatred? Hatred is usually preceded by anger. Anger rises as a reactive emotion, and gradually develops into a feeling of hatred. The skilful approach here is first to know that anger is negative. Often people think that as anger is part of us, it is better to express it, but I think this is misguided. You may have grievances or resentment due to your past, and by expressing your anger you might be able to finish with them. That is very possible. Usually, however, it is better to check your anger, and then gradually, year by year, it diminishes. In my experience, this works best when you adopt the position that anger is negative and it is better not to feel it. That position itself will make a difference.

Whenever anger is about to come, you can train yourself to see the object of your anger in a different light. Any person or circumstance which causes anger is basically relative;

seen from one angle it makes you angry, but seen from another perspective you may discover some good things in it. We lost our country, for example, and became refugees. If we look at our situation from that angle, we might feel frustration and sadness, yet the same event has created new opportunities – meeting with other people from different religious traditions, and so on. Developing a more flexible way of seeing things helps us cultivate a more balanced mental attitude. This is one method.

There are other situations where you might fall sick, for example, and the more you think about your sickness the worse your frustration becomes. In such a case, it is very helpful to compare your situation with the worst case scenario related to your illness, or with what would have happened if you had caught an even more serious illness, and so on. In this way, you can console yourself by realizing that it could have been much worse. Here again, you train yourself to see the relativity of your situation. If you compare it with something that is much worse, this will immediately reduce your frustration.

Similarly, if difficulties come they may appear enormous when you look at them closely, but if you approach the same problem from a wider perspective, it appears smaller. With these methods, and by developing a larger outlook, you can reduce your frustration whenever you face problems. You can see that constant effort is needed, but if you apply it in this way, then the angry side of you will diminish. Meanwhile, you strengthen your compassionate side and increase your good potential. By combining these two approaches, a negative person can be transformed into a kind one. This is the method we use to effect that transformation.

In addition, if you have religious faith, it can be useful in extending these qualities. For example, the Gospels teach us to turn the other cheek, which clearly shows the practice of tolerance. For me, the main message of the Gospels is love for our fellow human beings, and the reason we should develop this is because we love God. I understand this in the sense of having infinite love. Such religious teachings are very powerful to increase and extend our good qualities. The Buddhist approach presents a very clear method. First, we try to consider all sentient beings as equal. Then we consider that the lives of all beings are just as precious as our own, and through this we develop a sense of concern for others.

What of the case of someone who has no religious faith? Whether we follow a religion or not is a matter of individual right. It is possible to manage without religion, and in some cases it may make life simpler! But when you no longer have any interest in religion, you should not neglect the value of good human qualities. As long as we are human beings, and members of human society, we need human compassion. Without that, you cannot be happy. Since we all want to be happy, and to have a happy family and friends, we have to develop compassion and affection. It is important to recognize that there are two levels of spirituality, one with religious faith, and one without. With the latter, we simply try to be a warm-hearted person.

We should also remember that once we cultivate a compassionate attitude, non-violence comes automatically. Non-violence is not a diplomatic word, it is compassion in action. If you have hatred in your heart, then very often your actions will be violent, whereas if you have compassion in your heart, your actions will be non-violent.

As I said earlier, as long as human beings remain on this Earth there will always be disagreements and conflicting views. We can take that as given. If we use violence in order to reduce disagreements and conflict, then we must expect violence every day and I think the result of this is terrible. Furthermore, it is actually impossible to eliminate disagreements through violence. Violence only brings even more resentment and dissatisfaction.

Non-violence, on the other hand, means dialogue, it means using language to communicate. And dialogue means compromise: listening to others' views, and respecting others' rights, in a spirit of reconciliation. Nobody will be 100 per cent winner, and nobody will be 100 per cent loser. That is the practical way. In fact, that is the only way. Today, as the world becomes smaller and smaller, the concept of 'us' and 'them' is almost out-dated. If our interests existed independently of those of others, then it would be possible to have a complete winner and a complete loser, but since in reality we all depend on one another, our interests and those of others are very interconnected. So how can you gain 100 per cent victory? It is impossible. You have to share, half-half, or maybe 60 per cent this side and 40 per cent the other side! Without this approach, reconciliation is impossible.

The reality of the world today means that we need to learn to think in this way. This is the basis of my own approach – the 'middle way' approach. Tibetans will not be able to gain 100 per cent victory for whether we like it or not, the future of Tibet very much depends on China. Therefore, in the spirit of reconciliation, I advocate a sharing of interests so that genuine progress is possible. Compromise is the only way. Through non-violent means we can share views, feelings, and rights, and in this way we can solve the problem.

I sometimes call the 20th Century a century of bloodshed, a century of war. Over this century there have been more conflicts, more bloodshed and more weapons than ever before.

Now, on the basis of the experience we have all had this century, and of what we have learned from it, I think we should look to the next century to be one of dialogue. The principle of non-violence should be practised everywhere. This cannot be achieved simply by sitting here and praying. It means work and effort, and yet more effort.

Thank you.

GLOSSARY

Abhidharmakosha (Treasury of Knowledge) by Vasubandhu. English translation (from a French translation) by Leo M. Pruden, *Abhidharmakoshabhashyam*, Berkeley, California, Asian Humanities Press, 1991.

Abhidharmasamuchchaya – see Compendium of Knowledge

Arhat (Tib. dgra bcom pa) – to become an Arhat is the final goal of the Shravakayana. It is a form of nirvana, beyond rebirth, but falls short of buddhahood. The Tibetan word literally means 'one who has subdued the enemies', i.e. negative emotions.

Aryadeva – a disciple of Nagarjuna and author of many important commentaries.

Asanga – great Indian master, half-brother of Vasubandhu, who composed important Mahayana works inspired by Maitreya. He is especially known as a proponent of the Chittamatra school. Circa 4th century.

Bhavaviveka – also known as Bhavya, the key figure in the development of Svatantrika-Madhyamaka.

Bodhicharyavatara – see Guide to the Bodhisattva's Way of Life.

Bodhisattva – a being who has decided to bring all beings to enlightenment and who is practising the Bodhisattva path of the Mahayana.

Buddhapalita – circa 4th century Indian master, founder of Prasangika-Madhyamaka.

Chandrakirti – circa 3–4th century master, the greatest figure in the Prasangika-Madhyamaka school.

Chatuhshatakashastrakarika – see Four Hundred Verses on the Middle Way

Clear Words (abbreviated Skt. title: Prasannapada; full title: Mulamadhyamakavrttiprasannapada) – a commentary by Chandrakirti on Nagarjuna's Mulamadhyamikakarika. English translation of selected chapters in M. Sprung, 'Lucid Exposition of the Middle Way'.

Commentary on the Compendium of Valid Cognition (Pramanavarttikakarika) by Dharmakirti. No English translation.

Compendium of Knowledge (Abhidharmasamuchchaya) by Asanga. French translation by Walpola Rahula, *Le Compendium de la Super-Doctrine (Philosophie d'Asanga)*, Paris, Ecole Française d'Extrême-Orient, 1971.

Dharmakirti – famous Buddhist master of the 7th century.

Emptiness (Skt. shunyata) – the absence of true existence in all phenomena.

Enlightenment (Skt. bodhi) – purification of all obscurations and realization of all qualities.

Four Hundred Verses on the Middle Way (*Chatuhshatakashastrakarika*) by Aryadeva. English translations by K. Lang, *Aryadeva's Chatuhshataka: On the Bodhisattva's Cultivation of Merit and Knowledge*, Indiske Studier, Vol. VII, Copenhagen, Akademish Forlag, 1986; and Geshe Sonam Rinchen and Ruth Sonam, *Yogic Deeds of Bodhisattvas: Gyelstap on Aryadeva's Four Hundred*, Ithaca, Snow Lion, 1994.

Fundamentals of the Middle Way (*Mulamadhyamikakarika*) – a seminal text by

Nagarjuna. English translation by F. Streng, *Emptiness: A Study in Religious Meaning*, Nashville and New York, Abingdon Press, 1967. See also K. Inada, *Nagarjuna: A Translation of his Mulamadhyamikakarika*, Tokyo, Hokuseido Press, 1970.

Guide to the Bodhisattva's Way of Life (Bodhicharyavatara) by Shantideva. English translations include *A Guide to the Bodhisattva's Way of Life* by Stephen Batchelor, Dharamsala, Library of Tibetan Works and Archives, 1979; and *The Way of the Bodhisattra*, translated by the Padmakara Translation Group, Shambhala, Boston, 1997.[2]

Liberation (skt. moksha) – freedom from samsara, either as an arhat or as a buddha.
Madhyamaka – literally 'the middle way'. The highest of the four main Buddhist schools of philosophy. First expounded by Nagarjuna and considered to be the basis of Vajrayana. The Middle Way means not holding to any extreme views, especially those of eternalism and nihilism.

Mahayana – literally 'the Great Vehicle', the vehicle of bodhisattvas. It is great because it aims at full buddhahood for the sake of all beings.

Maitreya – the Buddha to come, the fifth in this present cosmic age. Many Mahayana teachings were inspired by Maitreya.

Mandala – the universe with the palace of a deity in the centre, as described in the Tantric practice of visualization.

Mantra – manifestation of supreme enlightenment in the form of sound. Syllables used in Tantric visualization practices to invoke the wisdom deities.

Mulamadhyamikakarika – see Fundamentals of the Middle Way

Nagarjuna – Indian master of 1st–2nd century CE who expounded the teachings of Madhyamaka, and composed numerous philosophical treatises.

Path of accumulation – the first of the five paths according to Mahayana. On this path one accumulates the causes that will make it possible to proceed towards enlightenment.

Path of connection – the second of the five paths according to Mahayana. On this path one connects oneself to, or prepares oneself for, seeing the two kinds of absence of self.

Path of seeing – the third of the five paths according to Mahayana. It is called this because one really sees the two kinds of absence of self, that of the individual and that of phenomena.

Pramanavarttikakarika – see Commentary on the Compendium of Valid Cognition

Prasannapada – see Clear Words

Samsara – the cycle of unenlightened existence in which one is endlessly propelled by negative emotions and karma from one state of rebirth to another. The root of samsara is ignorance.

Shamatha – 'calm abiding'. The meditative practice of calming the mind in order to rest free from the disturbance of thought.

Shantideva – great Indian poet and master of the 7th century C.E.

Shravaka – follower of the root vehicle of Buddhism (Shravakayana) whose goal is to attain liberation from the suffering of samsara as an arhat. Unlike bodhisattvas, shravakas do not aspire to attain enlightenment for the sake of all beings.

Shravakayana – the vehicle of the hearers or listeners, based on the teachings of the Four Noble Truths.

Sutra – the teachings of both the Shravakayana and the Mahayana.

Uttaratantra – the full Sanskrit title is Mahayana-uttaratantrashastra (Supreme Continuum of the Mahayana). This text is ascribed to Maitreya. English translations from the Sanskrit by E. Obermiller, *Sublime Science of the Great Vehicle to Salvation in Acta Orientalia* 9 (1931), pp. 81–306; and J. Takasaki, *A Study on the Ratnagotravibhaga*, Rome, ISMEO, 1966. English translation from the Tibetan by Ken and Katia Holmes, The Changeless Nature, Dumfriesshire, Karma Drubgyud Darjay Ling, 1985.

Vajrayana – literally 'the diamond vehicle', also known as Tantrayana.

Vasubandhu – great Indian master, brother of Asanga, who composed classic philosophical works on the Sarvastivada, Sautrantika and Chittamatra doctrines.

Vipashyana – clear insight meditation.

RECOMMENDED READING

The Dalai Lama, *The World of Tibetan Buddhism* (translated by Thubten Jinpa), Wisdom, Boston, 1995

The Dalai Lama, *The Meaning of Life from a Buddhist Perspective* (translated and edited by Jeffrey Hopkins), Wisdom, 1992

Jeremy Hayward and Francisco J Varela (ed.), *Gentle Bridges Conversations with the Dalai Lama on the Sciences of the Mind*, Shambhala, USA, 1992

Geshe Lhundup Sopa and Jeffrey Hopkins (ed.), *Cutting Through Appearances: Practice and Theory of Tibetan Buddhism*, Snow Lion, New York, 1989

Jamgön Kongtrul, *Myriad World*, Snow Lion, 1995

RECOMMENDED READING

H.H. Dilgo Khyentse Rinpoche, *Pure Appearance: Development and Completion Stages in Vajrayana Practice*, Snow Lion, 1996

Notes

Introduction

1. The first gathering to bring together leaders of the major world faiths and environmental leaders took place in Assisi, Italy, in 1986 and was organized by the Worldwide Fund for Nature.

2. 'No-soul' and 'no-self' are translations of the Sanskrit term, *anatman*. This theory is the third of the Four Seals which distinguish Buddhism from other philosophies and religions. The Four Seals are: all composite phenomena are impermanent; all contaminated phenomena are by nature unsatisfactory; all phenomena are empty of self-existence; and nirvana is true peace.

3. Dependent origination, or dependent arising, are translations of the Sanskrit *pratitya-samutpada*. It is the natural law that all

phenomena arise 'dependent upon' their own causes 'in connection with' their individual conditions. Everything arises exclusively due to and dependent upon the coincidence of causes and conditions without which they cannot possibly appear.

4. A buddha is literally someone who is awakened (from Sanskrit *bodhi*, awake) so buddhahood is the awakened state.

5. 'Cessation' is a technical term meaning 'the complete cessation of suffering'. Samsara refers to the cycle of suffering, and the cessation of that cycle is commonly identified as nirvana.

6. See *Majjhima Nikaya I*, p. 190–191, Pali Text Society. See also the *Pratityamutpada Sutra*.

7. The Ten Non-virtuous Actions we should avoid are: killing, stealing, sexual misconduct (three of the body); lying, slander, irresponsible chatter, verbal abuse (four of speech); covetousness, vindictiveness, and holding wrong views (three of the mind).

CHAPTER ONE

1. The Changeless Nature, translation of the *Uttaratantra* by Ken and Katia Holmes,

Karma Drubgyud Darjay Ling, UK, 1985. Page 135. The *Uttaratantra* is also known as the *Ratnagotravibhaga*.

2.   The Twelve Links of Dependent Origination form the twelve-fold cycle of causal connections which binds beings to samsaric existence and thus perpetuates suffering. These Links are depicted around the famous Buddhist Wheel of Life, which illustrates the six realms of samsara and their various causes. The Links are, going clockwise around the Wheel: ignorance, volition or karmic formations, consciousness, name and form, the six bases of consciousness, contact, feeling, desire, attachment, becoming, birth, and old age and death. See *The Meaning of Life from a Buddhist Perspective* by His Holiness the Dalai Lama, translated and edited by Jeffrey Hopkins, Wisdom Publications, 1992.

CHAPTER TWO

1.   For a detailed treatment of Buddhist cosmology in English, see *Myriad Worlds* by Jamgon Kongtrul, Snow Lion, 1995.

2.   The human world is part of the Desire Realm. The Formless Realm is more subtle than the

Form Realm, which in turn is more subtle than the Desire Realm.

3. The early teachings of Buddhism are divided into the Vinaya, or code of discipline, the Sutras, or discourses of the Buddha, and the Abhidharma which is the commentarial and philosophical literature composed by Buddhist masters. Two complete corpuses of Abhidharma literature have survived to the present day: that of the Theravada school, in Pali, and that of the Sarvastivada school, in Sanskrit. Only the Sarvastivadin Abhidharma was taught in Tibet. The chief reference on cosmology is Chapter Three of Vasubandhu's *Abhidharmakosha*, translated into English by Leo Pruden, Asian Humanities Press, Berkeley California, 1991.

4. Three Aspects of the Path, verse 7. See Robert Thurman's *Life and Teachings of Tsongkhapa*, Library of Tibetan Works and Archives, Dharamsala, India, 1982.

5. According to Tibetan Buddhism there are six realms in samsara, each dominated by a particular mental poison. They are: the hell realms (anger), the animal realm (ignorance), the realm of pretas or hungry ghosts (miserliness), the human realm (desire), the demi-god or Asura realm (jealousy), and the god realm (pride).

6. This statement can be found in *Majjhima Nikaya I* (p. 262, Pali Text Society) and *Majjhima III* (p. 43, Pali Text Society) and *Samyutta Nikaya II* (p. 28, Pali Text Society).

7. Buddhist psychology bases the perception process on six sense faculties: sight, hearing, smell, taste, touch and thought. Each faculty relates to a sense organ (eye, ear, nose, tongue, body, mind) and to a consciousness which functions specifically with that organ. There are thus six sense consciousnesses, the sixth one being the mental consciousness.

CHAPTER THREE

1. The term 'karma' comes from the Sanskrit word 'karman', meaning 'action'. It has three main meanings in Indian philosophy. The first is karma as ritual action, namely the sacrifice, in the early Vedas and Mimamsa philosophy. The second is karma as a particular category of human action, namely defiled and limited action, which we find in Samkhya Yoga, Advaita, the Bhagavad Gita and Buddhism. And the third meaning refers to karma not as an action but as a theory of action, in particular the theory of action as

causal determinant. It is to this third meaning that the Dalai Lama refers here.

2. *Chatuhshatakashastrakarika*, chapter 8, verse 15.

3. See in particular the third and fourth chapters in Vasubandhu's *Abhidharmakosha*.

4. See a fuller discussion of this topic by His Holiness the Dalai Lama in dialogue with David Bohm in *Dialogues with Scientists and Sages: The Search for Unity*, edited by Renée Weber (Routledge and Kegan Paul, London, 1986).

CHAPTER FOUR

1. The third category of phenomena are 'very obscure phenomena', which are beyond ordinary direct perception and logical inference. Generally, they can only be established on the basis of another's testimony or through scriptural authority.

2. This view is held in particular by the Shravakayana schools, especially the Vaibhasikas or Sarvastivadins, and the Sautrantikas.

3. Chapter XXIV, verse 18.

4. His Holiness is referring to a text known as *The Interwoven Praise* (sPal mar bstod pa),

which is a commentary in verse on Tsong-khapa's famous *Praise to the Buddha for his teachings on Dependent Origination* (rTen 'brel bstod pa). Lodrö Gyatso was a late nineteenth century Gelug master from Amdo and was more widely known as Chone Lama Rinpoche.

CHAPTER FIVE

1. See the *Dasabhumika Sutra* for an explanation of the stages of the bodhisattva path.

2. In the Indian tradition, the Buddhist path was generally presented as the Noble Eightfold Path, which is composed of: right view, right intention, right speech, right action, right livelihood, right effort, right meditation, and right concentration. The Tibetan tradition also describes the Buddhist path in terms of the Five Paths, which are the path of accumulation, the path of connection, the path of seeing, the path of meditation, and the path of no more learning. Within this framework, the Noble Eightfold Path would be included in the path of meditation.

3. The Bodhicharyavatara by Shantideva, X.55.